MORE FROM MARK DAVID GERSON

SELF-HELP & PERSONAL GROWTH

The Way of the Fool: How to Stop Worrying About Life and Start Living It

*The Way of the Imperfect Fool: How to Bust the Addiction to Perfection
That's Stifling Your Success*

*The Way of the Abundant Fool: How to Bust Free of "Not Enough"
and Break Free into Prosperity (coming soon!)*

The Book of Messages: Writings Inspired by Melchizedek

MEMOIR

Acts of Surrender: A Writer's Memoir

Dialogues with the Divine: Encounters with My Wisest Self

Pilgrimage: A Fool's Journey

FICTION

The MoonQuest

The StarQuest

The SunQuest

The Bard of Bryn Doon

The Lost Horse of Bryn Doon (coming soon!)

The Sorcerer of Bryn Doon (coming soon!)

Sara's Year

After Sara's Year

The Emmeline Papers

from Memory to Memoir

Writing the Stories of Your Life

Mark David Gerson

From Memory to Memoir: Writing the Stories of Your Life

First Edition 2014. Second Edition 2019.

Published by MDG Media International
2370 W. State Route 89a
Suite 11-210
Sedona, AZ 86336

www.mdgmediainternational.com

ISBN: 978-1-950189-00-7

Cover Photograph: Kathleen Messmer
www.kathleenmessmer.com

Author Photograph: Kevin Truong
www.kevintruong.com

More information on the author
www.markdavidgerson.com

One cannot choose what he writes — one can only choose to face it.
LUIGI PIRANDELLO

To the lives we live, the memories we share and the stories we tell. May they continue to inspire us and all those we touch. And to my daughter, who is always an inspiration.

Contents

Opening Words

*"It is your story to tell. It is for you to fix it in ink,
to set the truth down for all to read."*

The MoonQuest

I BEGAN WRITING MY MEMOIR in 2009, a few days after having facilitated a memoir-writing workshop. I had taught memoir-writing for nearly a decade by that point, but I had never felt any call to set down my stories. That changed moments after the last student left the room.

Suddenly and without warning, I knew it was time to write a memoir. My Muse had spoken, and as Toshar did with Na'an in my novel *The MoonQuest*, I wasn't happy with what I heard. Who, I asked repeatedly, would care about my personal stories? Perhaps, had I known back then that my memoir's title would be *Acts of Surrender*, I might have seen the cosmic joke and given in more gracefully. Perhaps, had I seen the parallel with *The MoonQuest*'s theme and story sooner, I might have been more pliant. Muses, though, are nothing if not persistent and, in the end, my resistance proved futile...as it always does.

Ironically, the challenge I faced when beginning *Acts of Surrender* was similar to the one I had encountered with *The MoonQuest*: I did not know the story. Oh, I knew my story or, at least, my version of it. After all, I had lived it. What I didn't know was the book's shape, structure or theme. How could I begin to write without knowing those things? Without knowing those things, how could I condense more than a half century's living into a compelling, manageably sized narrative?

We'll talk more about outlines later in these pages. For now, let's simply say that starting with an outline was out of the question. Even in high school, when I was required to submit one with an essay, I wrote the essay first and crafted the outline afterward. Without knowing it, I was already conceiving a writing philosophy I would not consciously connect with for nearly two decades: Just start and let the story reveal itself in the writing.

Could I do that in a nonfiction memoir with the same success I had achieved in novel and screenplay? Could I trust that my memoir was its own entity separate from the story I had lived and that it knew more about itself than I did? Could I surrender to that superior wisdom?

Perhaps the more appropriate question was, How could I not?

Of course, I would have to write a book of my stories in the same way I had lived them: from a place of surrender, trusting that the story of my memoir would reveal itself to me in the writing of it, just as the story of my life has revealed itself to me in the living of it. In other words, how could *Acts of Surrender* be anything but another act of surrender?

In the end, if you let it, an act of surrender is what every memoir is. It's what every book is: a guided journey where your Muse or your story or your unconscious or whatever you choose to call your creative source is at once travel agent, tour guide, navigator and driver.

That has been my experience through nearly than three decades of teaching, as well as through, now, nearly two dozen books, four screen-plays and three stage musicals-in-progress. It is that experience that I am excited to share with you through the pages ahead.

This is not a step-by-step memoir-writing how-to. When it comes to creativity, I don't believe in step-by-step how-to's nor, as you will discover, in rules. Rather, it's a writerly voyage that will awaken you to facets of your story you didn't know you knew and will *re*awaken you to the intuitive wisdom and creative power you already possess and that is as natural to you as is your DNA.

It's that power that will write your memoir for you, if you let it. It's that wisdom that, if you surrender to it, will transform your memories into a memoir that eloquently reflects the depth, insight and richness of your life and your stories.

May the alchemy of our time together reignite that wisdom and power within you and may it birth the memoir you have come to these pages to write.

Mark David Gerson
May 2014

Why a Second Edition?

A writer never knows, when rereading work that's more than a couple of years old, whether or not it still "fits." After all, authors grow and evolve but their books hover in a single moment in time, photographs snapped the day the final period drops on their final draft.

So I approached the first edition of *From Memory to Memoir* with a tiny bit of trepidation, wondering whether I would publish it as eagerly today as I did five years ago. I was relieved to discover that I would, unhesitatingly.

At the same time, I felt that there were tweaks and additions I could make that would take that five-year-old "photograph" and make it current. The result is this revised edition.

What has changed? I have developed new exercises and meditations and have either fine-tuned or expanded existing ones. I have included more tools for editing your memoir. I have reorganized some of the original edition's material for clarity and better flow. I even caught a few of the typos that slipped into that first edition, although I can't promise that new ones haven't weaseled their way into this one!

With these major additions and a host of minor ones, this second edition is about ten percent longer than the first and, I hope, at least ten percent more effective!

It certainly has been for me, reentering my life at the perfect moment, as I contemplate expanding and updating my own memoir. May it be equally so for you as, through its pages, you unleash your creative potential and transform your memories into memoir.

Mark David Gerson
January 2019

1. Getting Started

To be a human is to constantly weave stories.
DR. ANNE FOERST

Every "true" memoir must be incomplete;
what I remember may not be "true";
and people who know me may disagree with what I recollect.
TOM GRIMES

Your Life, Your Story

YOU ARE A STORYTELLER — not because you are unusual (though your experiences may well be), but because we are all storytellers. We each carry an infinite potential for self-expression-through-story that, if we open to it, can reshape our lives and the lives of others in ways we cannot begin to imagine.

In a sense, we are also all memoirists. From the moment the first caveman returned from a day's hunting and grunted his experiences to his mates over the cooking fire, we have been not only telling stories, but telling our story. From the moment of our first newborn gurgle, we have been communicating something of our brief life. From the moment the first diary entry reflected back on days, months or years past, we have been unconsciously crafting memoir.

Yet writing a memoir involves more than reciting dates, facts and what-happened-next's. A memoir is an intimate journey into what underlies those dates, facts and occurrences.

A memoir is also not autobiography. Autobiographies are vast and encyclopedic. Even should it span your life from conception until last week, a memoir is both more subjective and less comprehensive than any autobiography. Like an Impressionist painting, it includes more shade and texture than detail, more personality than panorama.

Nor is a memoir simply a published journal. While it may draw on your journals and may even quote from them, a memoir is more focused and less self-indulgent. It's a story built, however unconsciously, around a theme. It's a story that transforms the personal into the universal. It's a recounting of your experiences that transcends your experiences. It's a story designed to be shared.

Perhaps you have come to this book willingly — in order to leave a legacy for your children or grandchildren. Perhaps you hope to communicate your story to a larger audience — to strangers, as well as to family and friends. Or perhaps you come to this memoir-writing journey, as I did to mine, reluctantly, doubtfully, skeptically. Perhaps you don't believe you have stories worth sharing, stories that others would want to read, stories with the potential to inspire.

Of course you do. We all do.

Here's the thing: What you have lived is unique. What you have learned through your years of living is beyond price. And the value of all you share through your words, and of all the ways you awaken and grow through your words, is incalculable.

It's true for you. It's true for me. It's true for everyone.

It doesn't matter whether you are eager or resistant, overflowing with anecdotes or unsure where to find yours. Whoever you are, whatever your experiences, whatever your perceived writing ability, *From Memory to Memoir* will connect you with the stories you remember and, perhaps even more important, with the stories you have forgotten...with the stories you are keen to tell and, perhaps even more powerfully, with the stories you are reluctant to reveal. It will serve up the inspiration guaranteed to get you writing and keep you writing, the tools and techniques guaranteed to help you craft a rich, compelling narrative, and the support guaranteed to sustain you from the initial word of your book's first draft to the final word of its ultimate draft.

That's why you are here. That's why I am here.

So what are you waiting for? Turn the page and join me on this adventure of a lifetime...this journey into the experience of your own creativity as, together, we write the stories of *your* life.

How to Use This Book

If you have read any of my other books for writers, you will find some familiar guidance in these pages — not only in this chapter but through the book. That shouldn't surprise you. If you are even somewhat familiar with my approach to writing and creativity, you will know that it applies universally, regardless of form, genre or medium. My first "rule," for example — that there are *no* rules — is as relevant to memoir-writing as it is to fiction. It's equally relevant to your journey with this book.

For that reason, it would be hypocritical for me to insist that you travel these pages as they are presented to you. After all, I didn't write them in this order (any more than you may find yourself writing your memoir in order). In this as in all aspects of your creative journey, trust your intuition. Trust it to guide you from Page 1 through to the end of this book if that feels right or, should some seemingly random skip-about feel more appropriate, trust that.

All I suggest is that you visit the next section, "First Principles," early in your explorations, as it presents the philosophies that lie at the heart of this and all my books for writers.

Also consider keeping a journal dedicated to our time here together. Use it, of course, for the exercises scattered throughout the book; it may prove helpful to have all those writings recorded in a single place. But your *From Memory to Memoir* journal can serve a deeper purpose.

Writing a memoir is often a profoundly life-altering experience as you revisit the old patterns, old personas and old emotions of your past lives. Let your journal be the safe haven where you explore the many memoir-writing moments that have no place in your memoir — be they joys or struggles, fears or frustrations, obstacles or insights. All these (and more) *will* surface, so give yourself an outlet that will help you move through them.

In this digital age your journal needn't be a written one. Keep an audio or video journal should that feel more beneficial.

Finally, this is *your* life and *your* story. As I will repeat frequently in the pages ahead, there is no right way to write it. There is only the way that works for you and, even more important, the way that works for your book. So trust yourself, trust your story, surrender to your Muse and read on!

Guided Meditations

From Memory to Memoir includes eight guided meditations that will help you more fluidly remember, deepen and weave the stories of your life. These are powerful, cutting-edge tools designed to make your memoir-writing experience more free-flowing and spontaneous and to help ensure that your readers find the resulting stories more dramatic and compelling.

How to Use a Meditation

- Record it yourself for playback.

- Have a friend read it to you, then return the favor.

- Get yourself into a quiet space and place, program your music player for five to forty-five minutes of contemplative music or nature sounds (depending on the length of the exercise) and read the meditation slowly and receptively, following its directions and suggestions.

If you prefer a more professionally guided approach, I have recorded four of the meditations included in *From Memory to Memoir* (along with an additional six that are not in this book) on *The Voice of the Muse Companion: Guided Meditations for Writers.*

- "Your Ocean of Stories" (Section 4: "Writing Your Memoir")

- "Vision Quest" (Section 6: "Envisioning Your Memoir")

- "The Spirit of Heartful Revision," which is titled "Let Judgment Go" on the recording (Section 7: "Editing Your Memoir")

- "You Are a Writer" (Section 11: "The Writer You Are")

Options

- Stream "Your Ocean of Stories," "Let Judgment Go" and "You Are a Writer" for free as a subscriber to Apple Music, YouTube Music or Amazon's Music Unlimited, or download the individual tracks from Amazon or Apple Music.

- "Vision Quest" is available only on *The Voice of the Muse Companion* album. Download it from the bookstore on my website (www.markdavidgerson.com/books) or from Amazon, Apple Music or CD Baby.

2. First Principles

If I write rapidly, putting down my story exactly as it comes into my mind ... I can keep up my original enthusiasm and at the same time outrun the self-doubt that's always waiting to settle in.

Stephen King

I never know what's coming next... That's why I go on, I suppose. To see what the next sentence I write will be.

Gore Vidal

Mark David's 12½ "Rules" for Writing

THESE SO-CALLED RULES, adapted from ones I conceived for my first book for writers, *The Voice of the Muse: Answering the Call to Write*, summarize my views on writing and my philosophies on creativity.

Although the list continues to evolve, its key rule never changes: It's always designed to remind you that the only right way is the way that works for you *today* and that nothing innovative or groundbreaking was ever conjured up by agreeing to be bound by someone else's rules or ways of doing things.

Look for my 15½ rules specifically for memoir-writing in the next section.

RULE #1

There are no rules: How can there be when creativity is all about breaking new ground and breaking old rules? There is no right way and no wrong way, only the way that works for you today, so...

RULE #2

Be in the moment: Focus only on the word you are writing. The next one will come if you don't worry about it.

RULE #3

Trust the voice of your Muse without judgment or censorship. It is smarter than you are and knows the story better than you can. Or, put another way, trust your story. It knows itself better than you ever will.

RULE #4

Be vulnerable: Write from a place of powerful emotion, especially the one you would prefer to avoid. Go for the jugular...*your* jugular.

RULE #5

Love yourself and your words...every draft.

RULE #6

Don't force your words into the straitjacket of your preconceptions and expectations. Free them to take on the form and structure that is theirs.

RULE #7

If you're feeling stuck, don't stop. Write *anything*!

RULE #8

Always go with first thoughts. Second-thoughts are judgmental, self-censoring thoughts.

RULE #9

You're not in charge, so get out of the way and let your story have its way with you.

RULE #10

Write: Commit to yourself as the writer you are.

RULE #11

Set easy goals and meet them. Set yourself up for success not for failure.

RULE #12

Empower yourself: This is *your* creative journey. Don't let anyone else hijack it.

RULE #12½

There are no rules. None. Never.

In the Flow with the Muse Stream

What is a "Muse Stream"? If you're familiar with terms like "free writing," "automatic writing," "stream of consciousness writing" or "morning pages," you already have a sense of what the Muse Stream is about: a wholesale, uncensored, right-brain outpouring onto the page. But while those other techniques are used primarily as personal-growth exercises or to prime your creative pump, the Muse Stream is also a practical tool that will get your writing project completed — naturally, spontaneously and without struggle.

If you surrender to it, the Muse Stream will carry you from the first word of any book or story in any genre all the way to the final period.

I have written all my novels and screenplays on the Muse Stream. I wrote my *Acts of Surrender* memoir on the Muse Stream. And I am writing *From Memory to Memoir* on the Muse Stream, just as I have done with all my books for writers and just as I have done with all my self-help titles.

In short, the Muse Stream is the free-flowing river of creative output that we all aspire to in all our writing. It's the place where writer's block not only does not exist but cannot exist. It's the place where doubt and uncertainty cannot survive. When we allow ourselves to reside there, it's the place where the words tumble unhindered onto the page as swiftly as the waters of a stream tumble down their channel.

The good news is that, contrary to conventional belief (and perhaps to your experience) that free-flow is available to anyone, and it's available in every moment on any project — be it a poem or short story, a screenplay or stage play, an essay or dissertation, a novel or...a memoir.

Not surprisingly, the key to that unstoppable flow is, well, to write without stopping.

Without stopping and without thinking.

Too often, we think too much when we write. We think and we worry.

We think about where the next word is going to come from. We worry whether we're writing the "right" word.

We think about spelling, punctuation and grammar. We worry about form and structure.

We think about things we need to research. We worry whether we might be offending someone.

We think about paragraph breaks, chapter breaks, coffee breaks.

We think and think and think...and we never stop.

Let's return for a moment to our swiftly moving stream. The water rushes from source to outlet in a frothy whoosh of easy flow, nothing impeding its forward progress. Now, drop a couple of boulders in its path and watch them hinder that flow. Drop a few more, and you no longer have any flow at all.

Each of your thoughts while you're writing can be one of those boulders. The more worry or anxiety linked to that thought, the bigger the boulder...and the bigger the potential barrier.

Here's what's going on: For the most part, we think with the logical, controlling, analytical, critical side of our brain and we write with the creative, imaginative, free-flowing, analogical side of our brain. And for the most part, when we do the former, we stunt the latter. When we stop to edit or research or engage our "thinking" mind in any way, we also give voice to our inner critic, that nattering monkey mind determined to control a creative process that by its very nature is uncontrollable.

Why am I telling you all this? Because I am inviting you to write the first draft of your memoir on the Muse Stream.

How? It's easy: Write without stopping.

- Don't stop to correct spelling punctuation or grammar. There is a time for editing, revising and correcting. That time is *not* in the midst of your creative flow.

- Don't stop to grope for the word that's on the tip of your tongue or to search for synonyms. Leave a blank space or type *xxxx* and keep going.

- Don't stop to structure your story, figure out its theme or organize its contents. Just write and trust that the innate wisdom of your memoir will reveal itself to you as you write.

- Don't stop to research perceived holes in your narrative. Insert a brief note about what's missing, set aside separate time for research and write on.

Write without stopping and no boulder will ever be able to divert your Muse Stream.

Read more about The Muse Stream in my books "The Voice of the Muse: Answering the Call to Write" and "Birthing Your Book...Even If You Don't Know What It's About."

If You Get Stuck...
Seven Ways to Get Unstuck

There are many reasons why you might find yourself stranded on a shoal in the midst of your Muse Stream flow.

For example, you could be approaching an emotionally challenging chapter, and parts of you might feel reluctant to dive into it.

You might be listening to your inner critic or frightened inner child, rather than to the voice of your Muse.

You might be afraid of offending a parent or sibling or spouse with what you feel called to write next.

You might be over-thinking this part of the story.

Or you could be finding it difficult to continue without additional research.

If you get stuck — it happens — consider one of these seven techniques for reigniting your creative fire and restoring your Muse Stream.

1. Repetition

Repeat anything to keep your fingers moving across your keyboard. Repeat the last word or sentence you wrote. Repeat the first sentence of the previous paragraph. Repeat the first sentence of your day's writing. Keep repeating whatever you're repeating until the flow starts up again, and it will. In later drafts, you can discard the words, phrases and sentences that have no place in your manuscript. Some, you might be surprised to discover, will remain.

2. Free Association

Like repetition, free association keeps you writing while tricking your mind into relinquishing control of the creative process. Start with the final word of the last sentence you were able to write and let it trigger another word — whatever leaps to mind, however silly. Let that word trigger the next, the next and so on...until the flow returns. And it will. Again, delete what doesn't belong when you get to your next draft.

3. JABBERWOCKY

"Jabberwocky" is the nonsense poem that Alice discovers in *Through the Looking Glass*:

> *'Twas brillig, and the slithy toves*
> *Did gyre and gimble in the wabe:*
> *All mimsy were the borogoves,*
> *And the mome raths outgrabe.*

When you're feeling stuck, a little nonsense can get you going again. Make up words that don't exist and write them down. Write anything to keep the flow alive. As with repetition and free association, your own version of "Jabberwocky" will numb your mind and free your Muse.

4. BREATH

If you are stuck in your writing, you are probably stuck in your breath. Has your breathing become shallow? Pause for a moment and take a deep breath in, hold it for a few counts, then let it go. All of it. Do it again. This time, write "I am breathing in" as you inhale and "I am breathing out" as you exhale. Continue writing your breath until you relax back into the flow. The key in this, as in the previous suggestions, is to keep writing without stopping. Any way you can do that will help restore the natural free-flow of your Muse Stream.

5. CHANGE OF FOCUS

Move on to another part of the memoir, be it to another part of the segment that's giving you trouble or to another segment altogether. Return to this one in an hour, in a day or in a few days — whenever you feel ready or after you have carried out the necessary research, if a research-deficit is what has stopped you. If you have stopped because the segment is emotionally challenging, perhaps it's time for...

6. Exploration

Journal on the Muse Stream to explore why you are feeling stuck. Let whatever emerges guide you back to your manuscript and back into the flow.

7. Diversion

Sometimes, it's just time to stop for a bit. Take a break — to research, if that feels right. Or do something unrelated to your book. Meditate or take a walk or a bath or shower. Go to the gym, go for a run or do some yoga, tai chi or other mindful exercise. Or read a book for pleasure. If you have other creative pursuits, switch gears and engage in another Muse-like pastime: drawing, photography, singing, furniture-making, cooking...or whatever will keep you in a different kind of creative flow until it's the right time to return to your memoir.

Discover more techniques to help you get unstuck in my book "Writer's Block Unblocked: Seven Surefire Ways to Free Up Your Writing and Creative Flow."

Your Story Knows Best

When people see the nice books with the nice white pages and the nice black writing, what they don't see is the chaos and the complete frenzy and general shambles that the work comes out of.

MARGARET ATWOOD

Every time I start a new book, I forget that Margaret Atwood's words apply as much to the writer launching a project as they do to the reader turning the pages of a completed book. They certainly apply to this writer.

Thing is, I never know much about the books I'm about to write when I begin. With *The MoonQuest,* my first novel, I could rarely predict from one day to the next where the story would take me. In some moments, I didn't know from one sentence to the next. The resulting first draft was a single chaotic chapter that rambled on for four hundred muddled, repetitive, inconsistent pages. By the final draft, of course, the story had sorted itself out.

Even when I think I know the story, I'm generally wrong. That was the case with two of the three books in my *Sara Stories* series of novels. Both took a dramatic turn from the planned and anticipated before I had reached the end of the first chapter.

I expected something different of my *Acts of Surrender* memoir. After all, this was not an imaginary tale I was recounting. It was *my* story. Right?

Wrong.

Well, sort of.

Every book is its own entity, independent of the writer. Every book has its own vision for itself, independent of the writer. Every book has its own imperative, independent of the writer. We as writers exist solely to translate the energy of that vision and imperative onto the page, to take what is invisible to the naked eye and make it manifest.

That is as true for memoir as it is for any other genre. You may have lived your story, but the book of your life knows *its* form, focus and structure. Your memoir knows *its* story.

A few years ago a visual artist came to me with the painter's equivalent of writer's block. She was sensing a new style and form birthing through her, but she didn't know how to access it. All she could do was stare at her blank canvas in mounting frustration.

"Your only job is to hold the brush," I said, "because that's the one thing your painting can't do on its own. If you get out of the way and trust the brush to move your hand across the canvas, your painting will reveal itself to you."

She did, and it did.

It's no different with your memoir.

When I began *Acts of Surrender*, I had no theme and no title. All I had was a mishmash of stories, my own brand of Margaret Atwood's "chaotic frenzy" and my own version of my artist client's frustration.

But if I have learned anything through my creative life, it's that the story knows best. Always. I have learned too that if I start writing, the story will show itself to me — in the writing of it. And I have learned that if I surrender to the Muse Stream, what will emerge onto the page will be more eloquent and coherent than anything I could have worked out intellectually.

Through writing *Acts of Surrender*, I discovered themes in my life that I hadn't known were there. By surrendering to *Acts of Surrender*, the chaos dissolved and the book's perfect form, shape, structure and title emerged, as if by magic. In trusting *Acts of Surrender*, the process was largely effortless.

In the end, the Muse Stream is about trust. It's about trusting that if you move from the driver's seat of your creative process to its passenger seat, you will free onto the page a memoir that is greater than anything you could have imagined. It's about trusting that your memoir knows itself better than you ever will. It's about trusting that the story knows best — the one you have lived as much as the one you are preparing to write.

The Spirit of Your Story, the Essence of Your Book
A Guided Meditation

Allow at least 35 minutes for this meditation and for the writing experience that flows from it.

Get comfortable and close your eyes. Take a deep breath in, and let it go. Take another. Let that go. As you breathe in and out, let your shoulders drop and feel the muscles in your arms and neck relax. Feel your whole body relax.

With each inhalation, breathe in more deeply and feel yourself breathing in to the essence of your memoir, to the essence of your creativity, to the essence of your creative power, to the powerful essence of you.

And with each exhalation, feel more and more of the tension dissolve from your body. Feel the anxiety dissolve from your body. Feel the emotional strain and stress dissolve from your body. Let your shoulders drop some more, and feel nothing but peace and calm envelop you.

Be in the moment with that peace. Be in the moment with your breath. Be one with your breath, so that the only thing you are aware of in this instant *is* this instant...is the essence of this instant and, within that essence of the moment, the essence of your story, a story that has called to you so strongly for so long...a story whose call you have now, finally, answered.

What is this story?

It is the story that you are now writing or will soon be writing. It is the finished story that already exists whole and complete in its own invisible realm. It is the completed memoir that is waiting for you to engage with it, that is waiting for you to trust it. That is waiting for you to surrender to it. Unconditionally.

So, acknowledge that your story knows itself better than you do, that your book knows itself better than you ever will. Acknowledge that and open to all that the story of your book and the book of your story have to offer you now through this experience.

Continue to focus on your breath...to go deep within. As you do, as you let your breath carry you deep into your heart and deep in the heart of your story, allow an image, any image, to bubble up into your conscious awareness, an image that represents the energy of your story, the energy of your memoir, the energy of your book.

This image need not make conventional sense. There's a good chance that it won't. The image could be a thing. It could be a color. It could be a person. It could be an animal. It could be a sound. It could be a feeling.

Whatever it is, let it bubble up into your awareness. Don't judge it. Don't censor it. Simply let it emerge and, whatever it is, be okay with it.

Be aware too that if this is a repeat meditative experience with this same memoir, a different image may emerge for you now than emerged last time. That's okay. Just go with whatever bubbles up for you today.

We are dealing with a nonphysical energy and with your mind's representation of that energy. We are also dealing with your evolving relationship with your story, with your book, with your memoir. It's natural for your imagery to evolve as well.

Trust today's representation of that energy. Trust tomorrow's too, if it shows up differently. Trust that whatever emerges whenever it emerges is perfect for who you are in the moment you intuit and discern it.

Now, before you begin to converse or connect with that image, if you haven't already, get a sensory sense of it. Use your senses to help you connect more fully and deeply with that essence, with that energy — with the essence and energy of your story and your book — through the image that has emerged for you today.

Get a sense of color, if there's color. Get a sense of shape, if there's shape. Get a sense of depth, if there's depth. Get a sense of texture, if there's texture.

Which other of your senses is awakened by it? Smell? Taste? Sound? Music, perhaps? Emotions?

Not all your physical and emotional senses may apply to this image, but they may. Or those that are not relevant today may be relevant on a different day, or in a different, perhaps unconventional way.

So what does this image look like to you right now, even as you know that it could change in the next moment? What does it feel like? If it feels powerful, don't let yourself feel overwhelmed by that power. Know that that power is you, and that that power is an expression not only of the book's essence but of your essence. Not only of the book's story, but of your story.

Whatever this image is, however you perceive it, whatever its qualities and characteristics, embrace it. Take it in. Breathe it in. Fully. And let your sensory and emotional experience of this image connect you more intimately than ever before with the energy and essence of the story that it represents.

It's time now to listen, to listen to that image, whatever it is. It's time to listen from a deep place deep within you, to listen with your heart to what your memoir, through this image, has to tell you. You might not hear a conscious message, but something will move through you, however unconsciously. Trust that. And trust that however you experience it is the right and perfect way for you right now.

So take a few moments to listen...

Now that you have heard, felt or sensed whatever you have heard, felt or sensed, it's time to ask a question of your story, of your book, of your memoir, through the intermediary of this image. So silently ask a question. Then silently listen for an answer.

You may hear your answer. You may sense your answer. You may get nothing clear or obvious. Even if your question seems unanswered in this moment, an answer will come in another moment, likely in an unexpected way in an unexpected moment.

Trust that.

Ask another question and wait for another answer. And another.

Before we complete this experience, your memoir has some reassurance to offer you. Listen for it, and hear or feel it in whatever way you hear or feel it.

Finally, let your memoir offer you some closing words, whichever words come, to help you move forward on the next step of your creative journey with it.

Listen for those.

Remember that you have been chosen to bring this memoir into the physical in the form of a book. Whatever that may feel like in some moments, that is one of the greatest gifts of your life. Be with that for a moment or two. And feel what that feels like.

Now once again, be conscious of your breath. Be conscious too that this process will not end when you open your eyes, but that the intuitive sensings and messages will continue in the hours, days and weeks ahead. Remain open to them. Remain available to them. Trust them.

Be aware now of your physical body, of the physical space you now occupy, as you let your breath return you to full awareness. And when you feel ready, taking all the time you need, gently open your eyes and be fully present, ready to jot down any notes or thoughts from this meditative journey you have just traveled.

To Outline or Not to Outline?

One of the questions I am asked most often involves outlines. Do I or don't I?

I don't. At least not consciously on the page.

For me the outline is an intellectual exercise that constrains my creative flow and throws mud into the sparkling waters of my Muse Stream. Worse, it places me in the driver's seat of a journey that I know myself to be ill-equipped to navigate on my own.

Remember: Your memoir knows its story better than you do. Remember too that if your story reveals itself only in the writing of it, thinking it out ahead of time strips it of all magic and serendipity and muzzles its potential.

Put another way, your memoir is a voyage of discovery and rediscovery — for you as much as for your reader. Such explorations thrive best when they are freed of preconceptions and unencumbered by rigid itineraries.

New York Times bestselling author J.A. Jance admitted to me a few years back that she has not outlined any of her fifty-plus books. I was stunned. Jance, of course, writes mystery not memoir. Surely, I thought, if any literary form were to require an outline, it would be something as structured and plot-driven as mystery. Not for Jance. She begins each new book with a dead body and then, with neither outline nor advance notion of plot or outcome, writes her way to "whodunit," how and why.

Stephen King's attitude is similar: "I distrust plot," he has said. "I do [it] as infrequently as possible."

I have outlined none of my books — not my novels, not my books on writing, not my personal growth titles, not my memoir. I haven't even outlined my screenplays. Rather, I have relied on an intuitive knowingness — about what to write and when to write it and, later in the process, about how to shape, structure, revise, hone and polish it through to its final draft. My intuition has never let me down.

If the Muse Stream is about trust, it's also about intuition. It's about recognizing that, at deep levels, we already know the story we have been called on to write. It's about listening to the innate wisdom and inner vision that resides in those deep places. And it's about trusting that wisdom and vision, unconditionally.

When we allow ourselves to surrender to that intuitive process, we don't need outlines. We need only one word and then the next and then the next, in the moment-to-moment unveiling that is the gift of the Muse Stream.

That doesn't make outlining wrong. There are no absolutes in creativity — no absolute rights and no absolute wrongs. Your responsibility as writer-creator is to be open to whichever tools, techniques, processes, rhythms and routines reveal themselves to you and to adopt the ones the work best for you. It's also your responsibility to not get stuck in any of them. Recognize that what works for you today on one draft or project might not be appropriate tomorrow on another.

The key in this as in all things creative is to serve the story not our perceived need to control it, which, too often, is what an outline ends up being about.

If you feel you must outline, don't treat the result as gospel. View it instead as a general trajectory from which you are free to stray — randomly, wildly, illogically and frequently. Consider, too, outlining on the Muse Stream, which is more an exercise in brainstorming than in point-by-point outlining. How? Go nonlinear with techniques such as free association or mind mapping and let the exercise be one of expansion rather than constriction, of revelation rather than rote. Or plant a Word Tree, using the exercise in the next chapter.

The Word Tree

A Word Tree[1] is a nonlinear type of outline, designed to open your mind to fresh ideas and new possibilities. Here's how to plant your own.

In the center of a large piece of blank, unlined paper, print "My Memoir" and draw a circle around it. This is the trunk of your Word Tree.

Now, without stopping to think, analyze, criticize or judge, write the first word or phrase that leaps to mind, whether or not it's logically connected to "My Memoir."

Circle your new word, link it with a line to "My Memoir" and continue — by quickly writing, circling and linking the words triggered by each new association.

See each circled word or phrase as a leaf and each connecting line as a branch in this Word Tree you are growing.

Continue free-associating in this way until you feel complete with a particular branch. Then either return to "My Memoir" or begin a new branch from any word or phrase you have already jotted down. Keep going for 5, 10 or 15 minutes, or until you have a sense that your Word Tree has grown to maturity.

Once your Word Tree is complete, scan the page — again, not with your critical or analytical mind. Do it instead from an open, intuitive, free-flowing place.

As you do, let a word or phrase bubble up from your unconscious. It could be a word or phrase that jumps out at you from the Word Tree or it could be something else altogether. Whatever it is, jot it down and let it be the kickoff to an experience in writing on the Muse Stream.

---

[1] The Word Tree is adapted from the clustering technique developed and popularized by Gabriele Lusser Rico in her landmark book, *Writing the Natural Way* (Tarcher/Penguin, 1983, 2002).

Now, write nonstop for 20 to 30 minutes, setting a timer should that prove helpful. Remember to write without pausing to correct spelling, punctuation or grammar or to hunt for the "right" word. Remember too that if you feel stuck, you can use the repetition, free association or Jabberwocky-nonsense tips in "If You Get Stuck" to reinitiate the flow.

When your time is up, set your writing aside for at least an hour. Take a walk or do something else unrelated to your memoir. Then, when you feel able to look at what you have written uncritically and without judgment, read it — with an open heart and mind — and see what it tells you about your memoir, yourself or both. While this exercise is not designed to produce direct content for your memoir, it may.

Return to this exercise any time you feel the need for a kickstart. "Fifty-Five Keys to Trigger Your Tales" in Section 4 can also offer up an effective inspirational boost.

Time to Write

When you write a novel, you write it all day long, not just when you're sitting behind your typewriter. You write it as you smoke a cigarette, as you eat lunch, as you make a phone call.

RAYMOND CHANDLER

It's four-thirty in the morning, not my favorite time to be awake, let alone to be writing. But I woke up thirty minutes ago with an *aha* for a section of this book that has long eluded me, and I didn't dare ignore my Muse's call. Instead, I reached for the iPad next to my bed and began to write.

I finished my jottings moments ago and was about to go back to sleep when my Muse urged me to continue by sharing my experience with you. And so here I am — still awake!

Writers, like on-duty doctors or police officers, are always on call and writers, as Raymond Chandler pointed out, are *always* writing. Muses do not keep regular office hours.

"What about discipline?" I hear you ask. "Don't I need a regular, butt-in-the-chair routine? If I don't sit down to my memoir at, say, nine every morning, how will my Muse know to show up?"

Let me answer the last question first: Your Muse is always present, always available and always ready. The question is, Are you ready and available when it is?

As for discipline, there are two types a writer can adopt: conventional discipline, or what I call heart-centered or "soft" discipline.

Conventional or "hard" discipline is rule-bound. It insists that you write at the same time and for the same length of time every day, that you have the same writing goal for each session...or both.

Hard discipline is disempowering and mistrustful because it

suggests that you lack the commitment to write and the discernment to know when to write. Hard discipline also suggests that if you stray from this strict routine, you will never get anything done.

Don't get me wrong. There is nothing wrong with writing routines. The problem arises when we begin to serve the routine, rather than having the routine serve us, when we are so married to the routine that it becomes more important than the writing, when the routine becomes a rut.

Heart discipline, on the other hand, is about discernment and intuition. Heart discipline is about passion and commitment. Heart disciplines knows no set-in-stone rules, times or goals. Heart discipline is fluid and in-the-moment. Heart discipline places your Muse and memoir in the driver's seat of your creative enterprise.

Heart discipline says, "Trust." Trust that when you sit down, whenever you sit down, your Muse will be there for you. Trust that all you hear, including that it is either time to write or time to stop, is true. Trust that all the words that flow through you on a given day, be they five or five thousand, are the right ones.

Trust that should your Muse pull you out of a deep sleep at four in the morning, it is because four in the morning is the perfect time to write whatever is urging itself through you to be written.

Like intuition and discernment, trust is a practice. Practice listening to what's inside you. Practice listening to the voice of your Muse and the voice of your memoir. Practice being available and on-call. And always keep pen and paper or a tablet, smartphone or laptop by your bed and at the ready for those late-night creative emergencies!

Ask Yourself These Questions

- How have I approached discipline in the past? Was it "conventional discipline"? How did it feel? Did I ever find myself beating myself up for straying? How could I have approached that project differently? More self-lovingly?

- How can I apply heart discipline to my memoir?

3. 15½ "Rules" for Writing Your Memoir

There are no rules for good photographs,
there are only good photographs.
Ansel Adams

There are three rules for writing a novel.
Unfortunately, no one knows what they are.
W. Somerset Maugham

1. THERE ARE NO RULES

2. BE HONEST

3. BE VULNERABLE

4. ABANDON CONTROL

5. SHARE MORE DEPTH THAN DETAIL

6. BE SPECIFIC

7. ACKNOWLEDGE THAT "OBJECTIVE FACT" IS FICTION

8. RECOGNIZE THAT "FACT" AND "TRUTH" ARE NOT THE SAME

9. BE THE STORYTELLER YOU ARE

10. DON'T LIE OR MANIPULATE KNOWN FACTS

11. YOU WILL MAKE FACTUAL ERRORS: GET OVER IT

12. DON'T CENSOR YOURSELF

13. OWN YOUR STORY

14. LET YOUR MEMOIR OWN YOUR BOOK

15. WRITE!

15½. THERE ARE NO RULES

Rules? There Are No Rules

THAT'S RIGHT: THERE AREN'T ANY. At least none that matter. You already know this from "Mark David's 12½ 'Rules' for Writing," and it's no less true when it comes to crafting a memoir. As a matter of fact, the more you delve into my work, the more you'll discover that my first rule for most everything is always the same:

RULE #1

THERE ARE NO RULES

Every life is unique. So is every experience of that life. Why wouldn't every expression of that life also be unique?

We have already determined that your story knows best, that it knows itself better than you do at this moment...probably better than you ever will. From that place, there are no rules to follow — no should's, no must's, no have-to's.

The only given is that you are writing an account of your life. I almost wrote a "first-person account" in that previous sentence. But I stopped myself. Why? While we expect a memoir to be a first-person telling, what if yours were to come out differently?

The MoonQuest, my first book and the first installment in my *Legend of Q'ntana* fantasy series, is a novel. It's fiction. However, it's also my story, even if that story is couched in fantasy. Not realizing that I was writing a metaphorical memoir, I composed *The MoonQuest*'s first draft in the third person. Only in the final pages of that draft did I recognize that I would have to rewrite it from the point of view of the main character, in the first person — because I had just told my own story.

Without that third-person telling of what I believed to be someone else's story, I'm not sure I could ever have found the courage to write *The MoonQuest*. Without that illusion, I doubt that I would have been able to expose myself so nakedly. And without those first *Q'ntana* books as fictionalized versions of my story, I'm not sure I would ever have been ready to write *Acts of Surrender*, the real-life version.

What if you need some kind of transition into memoir? What if what you begin as memoir ends up wanting to be something else? Can you jettison your expectations and let it? Can you trust in the innate wisdom of your story?

Even if what you write is memoir, it may not be the memoir you expect. If you are honest and surrendered in your writing, there's a good chance it won't be — either in form or in content.

Don't feel you must follow a predetermined theme, trajectory or structure as you write. Whatever memoir "is supposed to be" — whatever you think memoir is supposed to be — your memoir will be what *it* is...if you let it.

Write the story that wants to be written by you, that has chosen you to write it. Write it the way you feel called to write it, not the way you think you should. And give yourself permission to break all the so-called rules along the way — for writing, for memoirs, for everything else.

ASK YOURSELF THESE QUESTIONS

- What should's, must's and have-to's have I been carrying about my memoir?

- Which rules, expectations and assumptions about my memoir can I jettison?

- Is there anything else I'm holding onto about this book that I can let go of?

- For each question make a list on the Muse Stream and, without thinking, do your best to tap into answers you weren't previously aware of.

Be Honest

It's easy to use a memoir as a piece of revisionist history, altering situations, events and circumstances in ways that place you in the best possible light and, even worse, in ways that judge, undermine or devalue others.

That's not memoir. That's ego at work in the first instance, revenge in the second — which brings us to...

RULE #2

BE HONEST

It seems almost too obvious to mention honesty here, but it's not. Bookstore shelves (and litigation records) are filled with examples of books and authors who have ignored or flouted this rule.

Don't write memoir to defend, justify or aggrandize. Don't write memoir to wreak vengeance or wreck lives. Don't write memoir to intentionally hurt or harm. Write memoir to explore...to discover...to rediscover...who you are, what you know, the meaning of your life.

Be honest. Be honest with your readers, of course. But you can't be honest with your readers if you are not first honest with yourself. In doing so, you won't be writing what you know so much as writing to find out what you know. You'll be writing not only to remember events from your past, but to remember what those events felt like.

That depth of recall can feel scary. That's okay. In writing your fear — either as part of your memoir or in your journal — you will be writing through and past your fear. "Feel your fear," Toshar is told in *The MoonQuest.* "Then pass through it to the other side, where your destiny awaits."

ASK YOURSELF THESE QUESTIONS

- Where in my memoir am I not taking responsibility for my own actions and outcomes?

- Where in my memoir am I blaming, judging or otherwise portraying someone in a negative light? Where in my story am I being deliberately hurtful?

- Where in my memoir have I altered events, however subtly, to make myself look better and someone else look worse?

- Where in my memoir am I not being fair? Honorable? Honest?

- Where in my memoir am I letting fear hold me back?

Be Vulnerable

I was living about two hours north of Toronto on Lake Huron's Georgian Bay in 1997 when a series of Muse Stream-like writings began pushing themselves through me. Two, three, sometimes four times a day during this five-month retreat, an irresistible force would propel me to my journal, where I would release a flood of self-directed inspiration onto the page.

A few years later a similar series of writings, all creativity-related, would transform themselves into *The Voice of the Muse: Answering the Call to Write.* But these *Dialogues with the Divine*, as they dubbed themselves in 1997, had nothing to do with my creative process. They had everything to do with my life process.

"Walk the earth naked, clothed only in your truth," I wrote early on. It was a call that would repeat itself often over the next years, never more insistently than while I was working on *Acts of Surrender*. This injunction, as I write in the memoir, "wasn't about coming out as a gay man. I had done that more than a decade earlier with minimal fallout. It was about coming out as frightened, vulnerable and imperfect. It was about coming out as human."

RULE #3

BE VULNERABLE

Your vulnerability will move your readers, deeply. This is not about being a self-indulgent exhibitionist. It's about revealing who you are — warts, flaws and all. Share your failures as well as your triumphs. Share your fears. Share your heart.

Your vulnerability is a profound and powerful gift: It gives your readers permission to be vulnerable in their own lives.

If you are not prepared to walk the earth naked, clothed only in your truth, you have no business writing a memoir...or anything else of substance.

Ask Yourself These Questions

- Where in my story am I wearing a mask or hiding behind a false cloak of respectability?
- Where in my manuscript am I not revealing the perfection of my imperfect humanity?
- Where in my memoir am I reluctant to walk the earth naked, clothed only my truth?

Try This

No life is without its heartache, heartbreak and emotional challenge. These can be some of the most difficult episodes to chronicle...and some of the most powerful to share. One way to get past any resistance is to write a first draft in the third person, as I did unwittingly with *The MoonQuest*.

Which of your life stories pushes the most buttons? Which would you rather not write? Write it. Write it first in the third person, as an observer. Be as impartial as you can be and just get the story out.

Once you have a third-person version, rewrite it in the first person, inserting yourself and your emotions more directly into the narrative.

Or Try This

Another way to defuse the charge around an incident is to write it first as fiction. Alter as many aspects of the story and its players as you need to in order to feel able to get it onto the page. Change settings, time frames, ages and/or genders but keep your story's essence intact.

Wait a day or so, then revise what you have written so that it accurately reflects the real-life events and accompanying emotions and can find a place in your memoir.

Abandon Control

As writers we are always keen to control our readers' experiences. We want to describe a sunset and have every reader know exactly what we saw. Or, as we come to understand the deeper meaning of a major life transition — a birth, death or divorce, for example — we want to make certain that everyone understands it and its impact precisely the way we do.

These are natural impulses, and they come from a writer's innate desire to communicate well.

Yet not only is that level of perfect precision not possible, it's not desirable. So...

Rule #4

Abandon Control

Skilled communication is not about exerting absolute control over your readers. Skilled communication is about trusting your readers' intelligence and emotions and about giving them the space to have their own experience of your story.

From the first moment the first story was told, listeners were engaged more by how that story felt *to them* than by how it felt to the story-teller. As readers, we are no different. We don't want the equivalent of a brain-to-brain data transfer. We want the equivalent of a heart-to-heart connection.

Unlike data transfers, heart connections are not precise facsimiles. They are Impressionist paintings.

Don't over-interpret your life for your reader. Don't try to control your reader. Don't insist that your reader experience your life exactly as you lived it...or as you want them to relive it. Paint the Impressionist word pictures that free your readers to find in your life the meaning in theirs. Give them space, and let that space be what links your heart to theirs...and theirs to yours.

ASK YOURSELF THESE QUESTIONS

- Where in my story am I over-explaining? Where in my memoir am I over-interpreting my life for my readers?

- Where in my story am I telling my readers what to think or how to feel?

- Where in my memoir can I trust more and control less?

Share More Depth Than Detail

Unless you're a celebrity superstar (and even if you are), the power of your story lies less in its minutiae than in its emotion. We may wonder what fashions 'n fetishes our favorite celebrities hang in their closets, just as we may be curious about which they gyms work out in or what they eat for breakfast. But unless fashion, exercise and diet are integral to your story, your readers will find that depth of detail tedious and irrelevant.

Your job is to inspire, engage and involve. Your job is not to show off your encyclopedic recall of the tiniest particulars of your life. Meaningful specifics are important (see Rule #6). Meaningless trivia is not. Hence...

RULE #5

SHARE MORE DEPTH THAN DETAIL

Chances are you're not famous enough to attract the level of voyeuristic curiosity we all carry toward movie stars and other celebrities. Again, even if you are, what matters most to your readers is the Inner You, not the Superficial You.

Share who you are at least as much as what you have done. And as you share what you have done, do it in a way that reveals who you are... and how you have grown into who you are.

Be Specific

This may sound as though I'm contradicting Rules #4 and #5. I'm not.

Let's say it's 1967 in my memoir's timeline and I describe my father's car as "a rusty, mud-encrusted '57 Ford Fairlane." Doesn't that tell you more about my father than if I were simply to refer to it as "my father's car" or even as "my father's old car"?

Depending on other aspects of your description — of your house or your street, of the state of your father's clothes or his general demeanor — you could reveal much about your family and your family's socioeconomic status without having to state it directly.

What if later in the memoir I write about my sixty-eight-year-old mother's pristine, hot pink Corvette? That would present one view of her. But what if, instead, I have her driving a dun-colored Dodge? Wouldn't your view of who she is and what she's about alter radically?

RULE #6

BE SPECIFIC

A single detail about who in your story drives what kind of car can tell you more about that individual in a few words than several paragraphs of narrative description. Does he hold the steering wheel in a death grip? Does she chew her fingernails at every traffic light while looking nervously out the rearview mirror? Is her foot always heavy on the accelerator? Does he creep along the freeway — in the fast lane?

Shrewd use of detail and imagery will immerse readers into the worlds of your life in unrivaled ways. And it will accomplish it by giving your readers the kind of space I talked about in Rule #4 ("Abandon Control").

The key in this as in all things is balance and discernment. Don't use description gratuitously — to show how smart you are, to show how good your recall is or to pad your word count. Use it to reveal character — yours as well as others'. Use it to add depth and texture. Use it to tell a story of its own. As you grow to listen to your story and learn to trust your discernment, you will find the balance that best serves your memoir.

TRY THIS

Pick a story from your past — one you have already included in your memoir or one you plan to include. Instead of thinking about it in words, imagine that you are painting it as a painting or a series of paintings. What would you want your reader to see and experience?

Now, translate that picture into words. Use all your senses — spiritual as well as physical — to describe your people and places, your subjects and objects.

What are the colors — of eyes, cars, sunsets, buildings, moods? Are there original ways you can express those colors? By using metaphor, for example?

Name your birds, streets, characters, towns, countries.

What's the model of the car? The year? Is the interior cloth or leather? Squeaky-new or worn? Pristine or littered with greasy McDonald's cartons?

Describe foods, settings, backgrounds.

What are the scents and sounds? The textures?

Open to new ways of relating all these to your reader.

Paint your scene as an Impressionist artist would — with just enough color and detail to let your readers "connect the dots" and feel as though they are present in your story. Don't make it so hyperreal that it overwhelms them.

You'll find more tools to help you get specific in Section 5, "Crafting Your Memoir" and Section 7, "Editing Your Memoir."

Acknowledge that "Objective Fact" Is Fiction

In Akira Kurosawa's 1950 film *Rashomon*, a violent crime in rural Japan is experienced by four individuals: a "perpetrator," his two "victims" and an "objective" witness.

As the film progresses, each character describes what happened, and it isn't long before we discover that each description contradicts the others. It's not possible for any two versions to be true, let alone all four.

Which is accurate?

In his video introduction to The Criterion Collection edition of *Rashomon*, film director Robert Altman answers the question for us: "All are true and none is true."

How can that be?

RULE #7

ACKNOWLEDGE THAT "OBJECTIVE FACT" IS FICTION

In a conventional mystery or thriller, we often encounter conflicting versions of the crime as the book, film or play unfolds. By the end of the story, however, we nearly always find out which one is accurate. Only one is.

Life, in this instance, does not mimic art. In life, as in *Rashomon*, there is no objective fact. My sister and I grew up in the same house, yet we were each attached to conflicting versions of the same incidents. Each of us was convinced that ours was the accurate one! My mother would have had her own take on those same situations, just as my daughter will recall some of our experiences differently than I do, and her mother's version will be different still.

Even history is not objective fact. It's a story told from a single and rarely unimpeachable point-of-view.

Where war is involved, for example, it is nearly always written from the winner's perspective. What about the losers? What about a neighboring country that remained neutral? How would one nation's war stories differ from another's? Even if we were to focus on a single side in the conflict, generals and foot soldiers would view the same battles differently, as would armies and civilians, as would distinct classes of civilian. And as with *Rashomon*, some of those accounts would contradict the others — not only in opinion but in "fact."

Recognize that "Fact" and "Truth" Are Not the Same

Fact is the date you were born. Fact is the dates of the reigns of the kings and queens of England. Fact is the dates of US presidential administrations. Fact is the dates of World War II.

No, wait! From the American perspective, World War II began after the 1941 bombing of Pearl Harbor. Canadians and most Europeans, however, will insist that the Second World War began two years before that, in 1939. Some Asians might date the war's start even earlier, as there were related conflicts in the region that predate Hitler's invasion of Poland.

For that matter, even the calendar by which we measure those birthdays, reigns, administrations and wars is not objective fact. That's because there are many calendars. There's a Hebrew calendar, an Islamic calendar, a Buddhist calendar, a Baha'i calendar, a Chinese calendar and a Hindu calendar. There's an Ethiopian calendar, an Iranian calendar, a Somalian calendar and an Oromo calendar. And while the current Gregorian calendar (created on the whim of a Pope) is the de facto civil calendar in large parts of the world, its Julian predecessor (created by Julius Caesar) is still used in Orthodox Christian traditions. I wrote the original version of this sentence not only in 2014, but in 5774 (Hebrew), 1435 (Islamic), 1392 (Iranian) and 4712 (Chinese)...among many others! Hence...

RULE #8

RECOGNIZE THAT "FACT" AND "TRUTH" ARE NOT THE SAME

In the early days of my *MoonQuest* novel, before I had conceived its

StarQuest or *SunQuest* sequels, I knew that the book would need some sort of subtitle. I struggled for days but came up with nothing. Then, suddenly, the phrase "a true fantasy" leapt to mind. I knew it was perfect...even as I wasn't entirely sure what it meant.

It wasn't long, though, before I remembered that fact and truth are often at odds and that a "fantasy" that emerges from the truths of an open heart can be as "true" as any so-called fact.

While that original *MoonQuest* subtitle has been retired, it remains the perfect description of what is, in many ways, a "fictional memoir."

Whether fictional like *The MoonQuest* or factual like *Acts of Surrender,* what is most important in a memoir is truth.

Truth is what emerges from your heart. Truth is your heart whispering into your reader's heart. Truth is your soul merging with your reader's soul.

It's that truth — not so-called facts — that will move your readers to laughter or tears, that will touch your readers deeply.

Ask Yourself These Questions

- Where in my story am I hiding my truth behind a rote recitation of facts?

- Where in my story can I let my heart whisper into my readers' hearts? Where can I let my soul merge with my readers'?

Be the Storyteller You Are

Your memoir is not a colorless encyclopedia entry. More subjective than either biography or autobiography, memoir is an *intimate* telling of your experiences and emotions. It's intensely personal. It's a story.

RULE #9

BE THE STORYTELLER YOU ARE

Even biographers, as one biography editor once reminded me, manufacture quotes and conversations to give life to their chronicles and personality to their subjects. As a memoirist you have even more leeway to use dialogue and other of the storytelling devices of fiction (setting, imagery, plot) to help your narrative flow more richly and smoothly and, more importantly, to help reveal the deeper truths of your journey.

Remember Rules #7 and #8: "Acknowledge that 'Objective Fact' Is Fiction" and "Recognize that 'Fact' and 'Truth' Are Not the Same." Remember too that Rules #7 and #8 do not give you license to distort facts or tell untruths...which is why there's a Rule #10.

TRY THIS

Are you having a hard time writing your memoir as a storyteller might? Take an incident from your book, or one you have yet to include but want to, and write it as a letter to a close friend. Alternatively, describe the incident to your friend over coffee, a drink or a meal, recording your telling into the voice-memo recorder on your smartphone. When you reread your letter or listen to your recording, notice how much more intimate, spontaneous and human you are allowing yourself to be. Rewrite your letter for your memoir or transcribe your recording and rewrite that, retaining the natural free flow of the storyteller you are.

You *are* a storyteller. You are because we all are! So relax, get out of your own way and let the stories flow!

Don't Lie or Manipulate Known Facts

It didn't take long for author James Frey's 2003 account of his treatment for drug and alcohol addiction, *A Million Little Pieces*, to soar to the bestseller lists. It was dramatic and hard-hitting, prompting *The New Yorker* to describe it as "frenzied" and "electrifying" and leading Oprah Winfrey to choose *A Million Little Pieces* as one of her book-club selections.

The problem was that significant parts of Frey's memoir were not true. When challenged, Frey initially claimed that "the only things I changed were aspects of people that might reveal their identity."

Frey was later forced to recant, admitting that certain of his "facts" had been altered and embellished. The result was a major literary scandal.

RULE #10

DON'T LIE OR MANIPULATE KNOWN FACTS

Don't, as Frey did, claim to have spent three months in jail when you were only in police custody for three to five hours. While no one's memory is perfect, no one's memory is that faulty.

Be honest. It is unethical to knowingly distort, manipulate or embroider the facts to boost your memoir's dramatic appeal. Yet even as you avoid embellishments that you know to be untrue, recognize that the debate over what constitutes an "untrue embellishment" is certain to continue for a long time.

Again, trust your story, trust your intuition and remember Rule #2: Be Honest.

You Will Make Factual Errors: Get Over It

A memoir is a series of memories and personal impressions. Problem is, your memory is imperfect and your impressions are subjective.

Do your best to remember accurately. Then, use any relevant personal, family and other archival material you can find to supplement your memories: photo albums, yearbooks, letters, journals, etc. Talk to friends and family members, where appropriate. Go online to genealogy and local history sites, where relevant. Check in with your local reference librarian for other resources germane to your story. With *Acts of Surrender*, I found Google's map, street-view and photo searches particularly helpful...and surprising when they showed how fallible my memory could be!

Research what you can as thoroughly as you can, then let it go. You're not writing for *Encyclopædia Brittanica*, which is just as well, because...

RULE #11

YOU WILL MAKE FACTUAL ERRORS: GET OVER IT

There is no need to be anal about accuracy unless there are legal implications to your story or you are writing about well-known and well-documented events. In the former case, consider having your final manuscript vetted by a lawyer. In the latter case, remember that even well-documented events are subject to Rules #7 and #8.

In the end, if what you write is emotionally true, your readers will forgive the occasional factual lapse. Just avoid the egregious variety described in Rule #10 and remember Rule #2: Be honest — with your readers and with yourself.

Don't Censor Yourself

One of the questions I am asked most frequently at memoir-writing workshops is, "How can I say that?"

My response is nearly always, "How can you not?"

RULE #12

DON'T CENSOR YOURSELF

Perhaps more than any other genre, memoir is not about holding yourself back. Memoir, as I pointed out in Rule #3, is about "walking the earth naked, clothed only in your truth." Memoir is about being vulnerable and imperfect. Memoir is about being human.

Still, it's easy, when revisiting the stories of your life, to feel as though certain things cannot be said, must not be said…dare not be said.

Don't fall into the self-censorship trap. Instead, ask yourself the following questions continually as you write:

- What am I leaving out of my memoir for fear of embarrassing myself or offending someone else?

- What am I whitewashing or watering down to avoid being judged?

- What am I afraid to say because of what my parents, kids, partner, siblings or neighbors will think when they read it?

Whatever it is, it belongs in your memoir, at least in its initial draft.

Only by writing it all, as *you* feel it happened, can you honor your stories and can you honor the memoir that has called out to you to be written. Only by writing it all, however painful the memory or traumatic the event, can you begin to exorcise that pain and trauma from your emotional and physical body. Who knows? That act of exorcism may be a key reason why you are setting these stories to the page.

And only by writing it all can you then, in your revisions, discern what is appropriate and what isn't and shape your memoir's final drafts accordingly.

Don't censor yourself. Get it all on the page. Now!

TRY THIS

Write your most embarrassing story, the one you would least want to see in your memoir...or the one your mother would least want to read in your memoir. Don't hold back. It doesn't matter whether this story ever makes it into the final draft of your book. Maybe it will; maybe it won't. For now, just write it.

Practice telling the truth on the page, regardless of consequences, and feel the relief and release that only the truth can bring you.

Own Your Story

Rule #12 is all well and good. But what happens when players in your story — parents or siblings, for example — claim that you've got it all wrong and insist that you tell it differently...their way? What happens when they urge you not to write all or part of your story? What happens when they tell you what to write?

Here's your answer:

RULE #13

OWN YOUR STORY

Never let anyone tell you that you can't write your story, that you shouldn't write your story or how to write your story. And if friends and family dispute your version of events? That's okay. They can write their own version!

Remember *Rashomon* and its mutually exclusive descriptions of the same event by the four protagonists (Rule #7)? As in *Rashomon*, everyone you are writing about is certain to remember every event you are describing differently. There is even a term for those conflicting interpretations: the "Rashomon Effect," after the Kurosawa film.

Not only do you own your story, you own your version of your story, as well as your unique perspective on that story.

And if people are upset by that story and perspective? Part of writing your truth authentically is that some people won't like it...or won't like you because of it.

It happens.

Don't sacrifice any part of yourself, of your creativity or of your craft to fear-based people-pleasing.

There's a good chance that if you write honestly, you will push buttons. That's not only okay, that's great! You want your memoir to elicit an emotional response.

Write your memoir as *it* demands to be written. Which brings us to Rule #14...

Let Your Memoir Own Your Book

You and your memoir are individual entities. Just because these are stories of your life doesn't mean that you know the best way to shape and structure them...or even the best way to tell them. Just because you think you know what your memoir is about when you begin, doesn't mean you're right. As I wrote in "Your Story Knows Best," every book is its own sentient entity. And even though that entity is an expression of *your* life story, it's an entity that knows itself better than you ever will. You own your story, but...

RULE #14

LET YOUR MEMOIR OWN YOUR BOOK

"I didn't really know what my memoir was about until I finished my first draft," author Karen Helene Walker confessed to me about her award-nominated *Following the Whispers*. I had a similar experience with *Acts of Surrender*.

Your job, yes, is to tell your story; but it's to tell your story as the memoir-book would have you tell it.

At the same time, be aware that this book that is your memoir is a trickster: It will do whatever it takes to get the ultimate story out of you, even if there's trickery involved along the way. Karen began her book thinking she was writing one story. The memoir that emerged was more insightful and compelling than anything she could have planned or imagined.

Let go all preconceptions, assumptions and expectations about what your memoir is or should be, and trust that it will reveal its true nature to you in the writing of it. Let your memoir have its own life through you, and trust that your memoir's innate wisdom will weave the story that will best serve it, serve you and serve your readers. Surrender to that innate wisdom. Get out of your memoir's way (get out of *your* way) and let the story tell itself through you.

Write!

You don't have to know your memoir's theme or thrust in order to begin. You just have to begin. You just have to pay attention to Rule #15.

RULE #15

WRITE!

If this seems the most obvious of my rules, it isn't. Not really. It's easy to put writing aside in favor of research. It's even easier to put writing aside while you try to figure out what this book that is calling to you is all about.

There is nothing to figure out. There is only this word and then this one and then this one.

Write what comes as it comes. Whatever it is. You will learn all you need to know through the writing. If you let its sentences flow freely through you and surrender to it unconditionally, your memoir will reveal itself to you.

Don't wait to figure out what your memoir is about.

Don't worry about its direction, theme, structure or focus.

Don't worry about chapter breaks.

Don't worry about what people will think of it, or of you.

Don't worry about anything. Set pen to paper or fingers to keyboard and let your memoir perform its magic on you, without judgment or second-guessing.

Should the direction change along the way — or should the theme, structure or focus change — don't fight it. Surrender to the moment. Surrender to the story in each moment. Your memoir knows best.

In other words: Write!

Try This

Pick one of the stories of your life — any story at all as long as it involves you and at least one other person.

- **Part I:** Take 15 to 20 minutes to write the story on the Muse Stream.

- **Part II:** Write the same story again, not from your point of view but from the point of view of one of the other people present. Put yourself in his or her shoes and see the episode and your place in it as he or she would have. Again, write on the Muse Stream. Don't think about it and don't worry about "getting it right."

- **Part IIa:** If there was a third person present, write the story a third time, from that person's perspective.

- **Part III:** Write it another time — not as who you are now but as who you were when it happened. Write it in the first person and present tense. Write it *as* it's happening.

- **Part IV:** Write it once again as who you are now. This time, incorporate the breadth and immediacy you experienced in the previous versions.

Do you notice any differences between the Part IV version and your original account? This can be a powerful technique for adding depth and richness to any story in your memoir.

For a fuller, more guided experience, see "Your Time Machine: A Guided Meditation" in Section 5, "Crafting Your Memoir."

Rules? Oh, Yeah. There Are None!

It's been a long time since Rule #1, so...

Rule #15½

There Are No Rules

Memoirists are creative artists, and creative artists are innovators. Creative artists are trailblazers. Creative artists go where others dare not go.

Write what yearns to be released from you onto the page — not as others have done it in the past...not as others tell you to do it.

Write it as only you, with your unique history, voice and style can do it.

Write it as only it can be written

Write it as only *you* can write it.

4. Writing Your Memoir

Anyone who believes you can't change history has never tried to write his memoirs.
David Ben-Gurion

If you cannot get rid of the family skeleton, you may as well make it dance.
George Bernard Shaw

Now Is the Time

WITHOUT THE MAGIC OF WRITING, the magic of reading could not exist.

If you have a story in you (and who doesn't?), now is the time to listen to its call and to start freeing it onto the page. Now is the time to start your memoir.

Now is the time to write.

Your Ocean of Stories

You carry an ocean of stories within you, an infinite wellspring of exploits, experiences and emotions that sometimes only surface to conscious awareness in the writing of them.

Like the mightiest of the earth's seas, your storied sea is a place of magic and mystery, danger and delight...a medley of the known and the unexplored, a blend of the murky and the magnificent.

You dive into that ocean when you embark on a memoir. And like all the great explorers who have preceded you, you may think you know what you will find on your odyssey. Even as you will surely encounter the expected, this journey into your ocean of stories will often astound you as it reveals treasures long ago forgotten. It will also occasionally alarm you as it reveals memories long ago buried.

Don't let your ocean's uncharted depths frighten you into abandoning the adventure. Dive in. Dive into the memories. Dive into the remembrances. Dive into the ocean of your memoir.

You will not disappear into that ocean. You will not drown in its waves. Its waters will support you. Its waters will anoint you. And you will emerge from those sacred waters transformed in ways you cannot now imagine.

It is impossible to control the changes that will have their way with you through this ocean crossing, just as it is impossible to control the stories that pass onto the page as you write on the Muse Stream. But in immersing yourself in your sea of stories, you *will* be changed.

Why? The act of telling your stories, of converting your experiences to words on a page, is a revolutionary one. As a writer of memoir, you must be open to the possibility of those changes, without knowing what they will be or how it will all work out when you first set pen to paper or fingers to keyboard.

All you can do is recognize the truth of this moment, of this feeling, of this story, of this word...and move on to the next from a place of trust.

Trust your stories, and yourself — through each word and each sentence — until your page is alive with the wonder of creation, until you are in awe at the life of your creation...and at the creation of your life.

Your Ocean of Stories
A Guided Meditation

Allow at least 30 minutes for this meditation and for the writing experience that flows from it.

A professionally recorded meditation similar to this one is available for download or streaming.[1] See "How to Use This Book" for details on how to access the recording, as well as for tips on how best to use this book's meditations.

Relax. Allow your breath to slow and deepen, slow and deepen, slow and deepen.

Close your eyes for a moment and picture an ocean. Any ocean. Anywhere. An ocean you have seen or visited, or one that resides only in your heart.

Whichever it is, see that ocean stretching out to the horizon, seemingly limitless in its scope. Feel its infinite nature, its infinite depth, its infinite breadth. Know that every story you have ever written or will write resides in that ocean, just as that ocean resides within you. Know that every story you have ever written or will write is as real and alive now as the sea life that thrives deep below the ocean surface of your imagining.

See yourself now in a boat on that ocean. Open ocean. A large boat or small. It doesn't matter as long as you feel safe, as long as you're comfortable, as long as it's your boat.

Get a sense of that boat that now carries you, supports you, propels you forward. Feel the salt spray on your face. Feel the gentle swell of the ocean's ebb and flow. Ebb and flow. Ebb and flow.

---

[1] Search the relevant site/store for "Mark David Gerson ocean of stories"

Allow your breathing to align with that ebb and flow as you become one with this environment you are creating. This ocean. This boat. This sea of stories that stretches as far as the eye can see.

Farther.

If your boat is moving, allow it now to slow or stop. Anywhere. Anywhere at all. As long as you remain in open waters. Drop anchor or allow yourself to drift. It doesn't matter.

Now, in your hands is a net, a special net that scoops up not fish but stories. Stories from the vast undersea world that is the infinite reservoir of your memory and creativity.

Take a deep breath now and cast your net into this sea of your creativity, this sea of your stories, this sea of the stories of your life. Cast your net and let it fall where it falls, sinking wherever it sinks.

Take a few more breaths, allowing your net to settle. As your net sinks and settles, take a few more breaths, in and out, your breath following the ocean's swell. In and out. In and out. In and out.

Now it's time to raise your net. So do it. Raise your net and see what you have retrieved. What you have received.

Whatever it is is perfect. Perhaps what has emerged makes sense as a story, as part of your memoir. Perhaps it makes no sense to your conscious mind. It doesn't matter. Whatever it is is perfect in this moment. For this moment.

What have you retrieved from the ocean of story? From the depths of your creative waters? From the depths of your memory? From the depths of your past?

See it. Feel it. Sense it. Know it. Fully. And now, write it.

Fifty-Five Keys
to Trigger Your Tales

If you're not sure where to begin your memoir, if you have already begun and find yourself stuck, or if you just need a quick exercise to get you going, pick a writing prompt at random from "Fifty-Five Keys to the Stories of Your Life," which follows.

Feel free to play with the list: Alter or combine phrases, adjust dates/times/places, replace names, change genders/tenses, etc. Do whatever it takes to make the phrase more relevant to your life, your story, your memoir.

Write on the Muse Stream — without thinking, without stopping, without judging and without censoring. Let the words and stories emerge naturally. Don't worry where or whether they will fit into your final manuscript. Some will and some won't. Your job right now isn't to figure anything out. Your job is to write.

By the way, I call these "key" words or phrases because the word or phrase that launches your writing journey is the key that un-dams your Muse Stream and unlocks the natural free-flow of your creativity.

So dive in and let the Muse Stream carry you into the stories of your life!

Fifty-Five Keys to the Stories of Your Life

1. I was born...

2. I forget...

3. I always wanted [a]...

4. My father/mother never let me...

5. My mother was born/died...

6. School was...

7. My best friend...

8. The first time I saw a dead body...

9. I never/always...

10. My first crush...

11. I got my first job by...

12. I hated that job/colleague/class/school/classmate...

13. My biggest secret is...

14. On the happiest day of my life, I woke to...

15. The day I was most embarrassed/humiliated...

16. The first time I had sex/made love, I...

17. We were best enemies...

18. I was always jealous/envious of...

19. If only I hadn't _____, I wouldn't have...

20. If you could read my mind right now, you would/wouldn't...

21. When I was 10/15/18/21...

22. I hated her/him/it until...

23. Before I die...

24. On the worst day of my life, I...

25. My first bicycle/car/motorcycle....

26. I cheated...

27. My father/mother/sister/brother...

28. Can you keep a secret?

29. If only I had...

30. My biggest accomplishment/failure...

31. My uncle/aunt/cousin...

32. "Oh, shit.," I cried. ...

33. I was so scared...

34. On my favorite/least favorite birthday, I...

35. My best/worst time of the day/year is _____ because...

36. If I hadn't been born...

37. I always/never knew...

38. I love(d)/hate(d)...

39. I remember/wish I remembered....

40. I had to hide...

41. I couldn't hide, so I...

42. My first kiss...

43. My last kiss...

44. My best kiss...

45. The day I lost/found...

46. My favorite hiding place...

47. I wish/regret...

48. I don't regret...

49. She/he/they...

50. My body...

51. When I discovered _____ , I ...

52. The day I didn't get married...

53. My favorite song is _____ because...

54. I'm writing a memoir because...

55. Once upon a time...

5. CRAFTING YOUR MEMOIR

I am still every age that I have been.
MADELEINE L'ENGLE

You own everything that happened to you. Tell your stories.
If people wanted you to write warmly about them,
they should've behaved better.
ANNE LAMOTT

The Power of Now

THERE IS NOTHING MORE COMPELLING than being in the middle of a story as it is unfolding. That's why film and theater are such potent storytelling media. When we sit in a darkened auditorium, gazing through the invisible wall that is the movie screen or proscenium arch, it's as though we are spying through a giant peephole, experiencing life and its stories as they are playing out in front of us in real time.

It can be challenging to achieve that same immediacy in a book. Even when written in the first person, as memoir inevitably is, most books are chronicles of events past and most authors reflect back on what occurred long ago with the wisdom of hindsight but the emotional remove of time.

Present-tense accounts are rare for good reason: They can be difficult to write well and, because we are so accustomed to the past-tense literary convention, they can also be awkward to read.

So how do we bridge the time gap in our memoirs? How do we write about what occurred decades ago yet make our readers feel as though it's happening right now?

Here are three ways...

1. DON'T INTERPRET

It's natural to want to explain the stories of our life as we recount them. It's natural to want the reader to see our life as we *now* see it. It's natural to want to expound, explicate and elucidate. It's natural to want to interpret.

Don't do it! It's not your job.

When you interpret your stories for your readers, you're telling them not only how to read your book but how to read your life. You are not only setting yourself up as their teacher, you are trying to control their reading experience.

Did I mention that that's not your job? As I wrote in Section 3 (Rule #4: "Abandon Control"), you are not in charge of your reader's experience — in memoir any more than in fiction. In fact, you're not in charge of much of anything! Your job is to tell your story as it wants to be told. Period.

Trust your readers to find their own way through your stories.

What does that have to do with the "power of now"? Interpretation distances you from what happened in the past. Interpretation distances you from who you were when what happened happened. Interpretation strips the immediacy from your narrative and drains away much of its emotional potency.

2. BE CHILDLIKE

"Far too many people," author Madeleine L'Engle wrote in *A Circle of Quiet*, "misunderstand what putting away childish things means and think that forgetting what it is like to think and feel and touch and smell and taste and see and hear like a three-year-old or a thirteen-year-old or a twenty-three-year-old means being grownup. ... [I]f this is what it means to be a grownup, then I don't ever want to be one."

Can you be a grownup author and still connect with the joys and woes, passions and sorrows, triumphs and terrors of every age you have ever been? Can you not only remember who you were when whatever happened happened but, in a sense, *be* who you were? Can you, as my *MoonQuest* protagonist realizes he must as he is pressed to write his own memoir, allow the child you were to touch the adult you have now become?

When you allow yourself to enter into the sensory and emotional worlds of who you were *as* who you were, you free your readers to travel those same worlds with you. You also gift them with the too-rare opportunity to explore and reexperience their own sensory and emotional life through your words.

3. HOLD NOTHING BACK

You will be tempted to temper your emotions. You will be tempted to censor your experiences. You will be tempted to let your logical mind determine which stories to tell and how freely to tell them.

Send your logical mind out for coffee and let your intuitive mind guide your pen across the page or your fingers across the keyboard.

Go back in time and give your emotions and senses free rein. Feel it all. Touch it all. See it all. Hear it all. Taste it all. Smell it all. And then write it all, holding nothing back, especially in your first draft, where you are still discovering what your memoir is all about and where the words that spill onto the page are still revealing to you what your life has been all about.

Your Time Machine
A Guided Meditation

Allow 45 to 60 minutes for this meditation and for the writing exercises that follow it. If possible, complete all exercises in a single sitting.

Close your eyes and relax. Breathe in fully and exhale completely, letting each breath carry you deeper into yourself, deeper into that sacred, profoundly personal place where your creativity resides...where your memories reside.

Slow your breath...and slow it some more. Deepen your breath...and deepen it some more. Allow your shoulders to drop...and drop some more. And some more.

As your shoulders drop let your defenses drop. Allow yourself to relax. Fully. Allow yourself to open. Completely.

Allow yourself to be vulnerable.

Even as you allow yourself to be vulnerable, know that you are safe, safe in the enfolding cocoon of this experience.

You're calm. You're relaxed. But you're awake and aware. Fully aware. Aware enough to recall all that you feel, see and experience during our time together, aware enough that when the moment comes to do so, you will be able to set it onto the page, remembering even more as you write.

But that's for later. For now, again focus on your breath and feel that breath of life, your life, melt any and all knots of tension and stress in your body. Let every instant but this one dissolve and let yourself relax into it — into this instant...and now this instant...and now this one.

From that place of calm, let your breath transport you into the realm of memory, the realm of creativity, the realm of vision. And from that place, I'd like you to see yourself standing in front of an elevator door.

It can be an elevator you have seen before, one you know. Or it can be an elevator you are seeing for the first time. It can be inside a building or it can, perhaps strangely, be sitting outside. However you see or experience it is perfect.

We all visualize differently. Some of us see and hear clearly, as though we are physically present in the scene or watching a movie. Some of us see only in vague moving shadows. Others see nothing but sense everything through a kind of inner knowingness. However you visualize is perfect for you and perfect for this experience.

So you find yourself standing in front of this elevator door. What does it look like? Is it the sleek stainless steel or gleaming bronze of a modern skyscraper? Or does it have a more vintage look? It could even be wooden. Is it smooth or is it etched, carved or otherwise textured? Touch it and be aware how it feels.

What about the elevator's call button? What's it like? Is it a simple button, or does it have a light? What kind of light?

Are you ready to press it? Yes? Then do it, and feel what that feels like.

When the elevator doors open, step inside and become as aware of the interior of the cab as you were its exterior. Take a few moments to do that.

Whatever else is in the elevator cab, there is, of course, an instrument panel. But this is no ordinary instrument panel because this one has only two buttons: One is labeled PRESENT, which is where you are now; the other is labeled PAST, which is where you are going.

Press the PAST button and wait as the elevator descends.

In less time than you would think possible, you arrive at your destination and the doors open.

The doors open and you step out — into another time and place, a time and place where something happened. Something important. Something significant.

This may be an incident that you plan to include in your memoir. It may not be. It could even be an incident that predates your narrative...a piece of backstory. Go with whatever comes up, whatever it is, even if it ends up having no place in your final book.

Whatever the incident or situation, it has some charge to it, some emotion or emotions behind it. It could be a joyful or disturbing time, an exhilarating or terrifying time. It doesn't matter. You could be alone or with someone or in a group. That, too, doesn't matter.

Whatever it is, it's the perfect experience for right now, so don't run from it, however challenging you might find it. Know that in this as in all your meditative and visionary experiences here, you are safe. Know, also, that if anything gets too overwhelming, you can return at any time to your elevator, press PRESENT and let the elevator carry you back to now.

For now, though, step out of the elevator into that time, into that place, into that experience. Step into it not as who you are now. Step into it as the younger person you were when that experience took place.

To be clear: You are not an observer in this scene. You are a player, the principal player — at whatever age you were at the time. Step into that moment in your life and relive it. Fully. With any other player who was also present at the time.

Bring all your senses into the experience. All your senses and all relevant emotions. Be aware of what you see. Be aware of what you hear. Be aware of what you can touch. Be aware of what you can smell. Be aware of how you feel — again, not as who you are today looking back, but as who you were in that moment. Be fully present in that moment.

Pause the recording now and take all the time you need to revisit and relive whatever happened. When your experience is complete and you are ready, start it up again.

Your experience from the past is now complete. You have seen what you saw, felt what you felt and relived, as who you were, the experiences that called to you to be relived. It is now time to return to the elevator and to this point in time as who you are...as who you are today.

Before you go, though, pause to take in anything else of your surroundings or of the situation that you might have overlooked. Pause too to thank anyone or anything that might have contributed to your experience.

When you are ready, return to the elevator and press the call button.

As the elevator doors open and you step inside, you are now, once again, your present age and in your present body. But you have retained all the sensory and emotional memories of your past-time experience and will continue to retain them as you press the PRESENT button and the elevator returns you to this present moment.

You will recall even more detail in a few minutes as you begin to write about your experiences.

The elevator rises, its doors open and you step outside, back to your starting point.

Now that starting point, too, begins to dissolve, and you once again find yourself in the place and space where you began this meditative journey into the past.

Be aware, once more, of your physical body, of your breath. Slowly, begin to move your fingers and wiggle your toes. Lightly shrug your shoulders and gently move your head. Let yourself yawn and stretch. And when you're ready, open your eyes and feel yourself fully present.

Now, with pen and paper or computer or tablet at hand, follow the rest of these instructions, pausing the recording between exercises.

MEMOIR EXERCISE #1

Allowing the full range of emotions room to play themselves out, write about the events of your meditation as the person you were then. Write in the first person and present tense (I am). Write as though you are experiencing those events right now, not knowing what is going to happen next. Write your feelings and express them fully, holding nothing back. Use all your senses: What do things look like, sound like, taste like, smell like, evoke? Be as in-the-moment in your writing as you were in the experience.

Take all the time you need and when you are complete with your writing, continue (immediately, if possible) to the next exercise.

MEMOIR EXERCISE #2

Write the same experience again but in the past tense, though still in the first person (I was). Write it from the perspective of who you are now, looking back. Let all the freshness and immediacy you rediscovered in the meditation and in the first exercise find its way onto the page.

Don't forget to avoid interpretation. Simply tell the story as you lived it, using all your senses to describe the settings, places and people in ways that evoke your emotional experience and that take your reader *into* that time and place.

Take all the time you need and when you are complete, continue (immediately, if possible) to the next exercise.

MEMOIR EXERCISE #3 (OPTIONAL)

Write the same experience one final time, but in the third person past tense (he/she was). Let this detached perspective offer you fresh insight into the situation you are writing about, as well as into yourself.

As before, avoid interpretation and recount the story as it happened, bringing your sensory experiences of the first exercise into this telling as well.

Painting the People of Your Past

Whether you are writing fiction or memoir — or a magazine profile or biography — you are writing stories. And whatever your story, it's the people in it who will bring it most to life.

Even in a first-person account of an isolated time in the wilderness, you are still interacting with characters. It's just that in that type of story, your "characters" might be pets or wild animals...or objects. Story is always about character, even if it's the fish in *Finding Nemo*, the talking trees of *The Wizard of Oz* or the enchanted broom of *Fantasia*.

In a memoir, of course, *you* are the primary character you must bring to life in your telling. You do that, as I said earlier, by being uncompromisingly honest, by letting yourself be emotionally vulnerable and by holding nothing back.

What about your other characters? How do you ensure that they are as animated on the page as they were when you first encountered them off the page, in "real" life?

One way is through description: You can tell a lot about someone from his eyes, her smile, his hands, her walk. Clothing can be equally revealing. Think about what the style, age, colors and condition — even the fabric — of what someone is wearing might tell you. What about hair and, for men, facial hair? Or nervous tics or other unconscious habits?

A few words of description can suggest mood and character, can denote socioeconomic background, can hint at physical and emotional state...can drop readers directly into the world of your memoir.

Here are three examples of character description from my *Acts of Surrender* memoir:

> Charles was dark, heavyset and in his late thirties, unkempt
> in blue jeans and a rumpled white sweatshirt, not at all my

PlayGirl fantasy. But, then, I wasn't his. Compassionate and to the point, he looked me up and down and asked, "Are you Jewish?"

Back at Mount Royal High School, Faith Silver had been my freshman English, history and homeroom teacher. A spritely, red-headed presence with a passion for her students, she and I developed an early bond...

Carole was warm and nurturing, with an infectious smile that could melt any heart, even mine...although it would take more than a day's exposure to do it.

In each instance, it takes no more than a brief paragraph to present Charles, Faith and Carole, offer insight into each one's character and suggest something of our relationship.

In this introduction to another player from my past, I continue into a second paragraph with a snippet of dialogue that deepens my mini-portrait.

A few inches shorter than my five-foot-eleven and a few pounds heavier than my one hundred and forty, Ron wore a worn tweedy jacket and sported a graying beard and mustache. He grinned warmly and offered me a tour of the renovated farmhouse he shared with his wife, Carol, and their two sons.

"There's no front-door key," Ron said as he ushered me in. "Actually, there are no house keys at all. We lost them a long time ago and never bothered replacing them." He also confided that the key to his station wagon never left the ignition. "That way, I always know where it is."

Remember my memoir-writing Rule #9: As the storyteller you are, you are free to use a novelist's tools to help your narrative flow more richly, to flesh out character and to reveal the deeper truths of your journey.

Remember too your responsibility to truth. Don't misrepresent. Don't be intentionally misleading or malicious. And don't use dialogue and description as cudgels of judgment or revenge.

ASK YOURSELF THESE QUESTIONS

- Which of the people mentioned in my memoir comes across as flat, more like a cardboard cutout than a person?

- Can I find one or two details that will bring that character to life?

- Can I craft a few lines of dialogue that are true to the character and situation and that misrepresent neither?

TRY THIS

Next time you're out, watch the people around you to see what you can discern about them and about their lives from simple actions, behaviors and physical characteristics. Notice how they sit, stand and walk. Be aware how they relate to others. Pay attention not only to what is revealed but to what might be being concealed. Write a quick story about what you're seeing and discover how a few well-chosen details, judiciously applied, can enhance and enrich your account.

Reawakening Your Memory: The People

Use this checklist to trigger your memory about the players in your life story. This is not about answering each question for each individual; after all, it's your story you are writing, not theirs! Rather, it's an exercise in remembering qualities you might have forgotten and discerning which characteristics might enhance your story.

You can also use relevant items on the list on yourself as a memory tool — on the you you were at the different phases and stages of your life that are chronicled in your memoir.

Take notes if you choose, or let the list reignite your recall and rekindle your senses.

- First word or phrase that leaps to mind as you think of this person — both now and at the time he or she appears in your memoir
- Nickname
- Age / Age appearance (does this person look his/her age? older? younger?)
- Height / Weight / Body Type / Posture
- Nationality
- Face (shape, complexion, makeup)
- Hair (color, style, length) / Facial hair
- Eyes (shape, color)
- Hands / Fingernails
- Scars / Attitude toward scars
- Unusual physical characteristics
- Gait (how this person walks)
- Voice / Manner (soft? grating? blustery?)
- Language / Manner of Speech / Vocabulary / Accent
- Favorite expression

- Unusual traits, mannerisms
- Eccentricities / Odd habits
- Fears / Phobias
- Maturity level
- Clothing (style, fabric, condition)
- Jewelry / Accessories
- Profession / Employment
- Hobbies / Interests
- Schooling
- Unusual skills
- Greatest wish / desire
- Greatest regret
- Worst nightmare
- Favorite foods, drinks / Unusual foods, drinks
- Preferred reading, films, TV, etc.
- Attitude toward technology
- Favorite gadgets
- Pets
- Relationship with and/or attitude toward men, women, children, pets
- Relationship with and/or attitude toward family, self, you
- Favorite story about this person
- Random thought about this person

Character Connections
A Guided Meditation

Let this meditation help trigger your recall of specific events as well as your sensory memory of the people involved. Not every question or suggestion will apply universally, nor could an experience like this cover every potential detail. As with the list earlier in this chapter, ignore what is irrelevant and fill in whatever gaps apply to your situation.

Allow at least 35 minutes for this meditation and for the writing experience that flows from it.

Close your eyes and get comfortable. Allow your body to relax. Breathe in as deeply as you can and let it go. And again.

Breathe into the sureness of your power and empowerment. Breathe out all fear, all doubt, all judgment.

Breathe into your voice and your creativity. Breathe out anything and everything is not in alignment with that.

Let your shoulders drop, and feel all stress and strain drain away from them and from your neck, where we carry so much stress, responsibility and anxiety.

Feel the tension around your eyes lighten. Too often, we scrunch our eyes and foreheads, trying to focus, trying to see. You don't have to *try* to see anything. This is an experience in allowing...in allowing the vision to come, in allowing the real-life characters who populate your story to present themselves to you.

So continue to breathe, to focus on your breath, and let everything else go.

Now, from a deep place within you, invite someone from your story to come into consciousness. It could be someone from your immediate or distant past. It could also be you at an earlier age.

If this is your first experience with this meditation, I encourage you to not choose a specific person but, rather, to let the person who chooses him- or herself to come to you. It may or may not be the person you would prefer to talk to right now. It doesn't matter. What matters is that you open your heart and mind right now to the person from your past who is ready to speak to you.

More important than that, as important as that is, I invite you to trust whatever you feel, whatever you sense, whatever you hear, whatever you think you know but are afraid to trust. This is an exercise in many things; it is also an exercise in trust.

And so this individual, whoever she or he is, stands before you.

Because this is a generic meditation, I might pose some questions that could seem obvious or that might be irrelevant to a particular person or experience. Just because they don't apply this time doesn't mean that they won't apply next time. For now, feel free to ignore any question that is not applicable and to replace it with your own.

Be aware too that this individual might not be a person. It could be a pet or other animal. It could be an inanimate object that has come to life for this experience. Again, be open to it showing up however it shows up and free yourself to have the experience that presents itself.

Let's start with what is most likely obvious: What is this person's name? Is this individual male or female?

Be aware that this character might be present in your story at different ages and stages in his or her life. If that's the case, this experience is one of those ages and stages.

And so at this moment in your story and in your character's life, what is your sense of his or her age? Even if you don't know exactly, guess. Does this person appear to be older or younger than his or her age? Some people look and carry themselves as much older than their chronological age. Sometimes the reverse can be true. This is an opportunity to get a sense of what kind of life this person has lived by the connect or disconnect between chronological age and appearance.

At this stage in your character's life, does he or she have a nickname?

What is your character wearing? Is it typical dress for your character? For your character's age? For your character's era? For the time of year or season? If not, what is the significance of this outfit? And what would she or he normally be wearing at this time? Regardless, what is the quality of the clothes he or she is wearing right now? Are they new? Old? How do they fit? Are they pressed and clean? Or worn? Dirty?

Once again, you may get answers or no answers to some of these questions. You may see clearly or you may sense or intuit. It doesn't matter. Your experience, whatever it is, is absolutely right and perfect.

Look at your character's hair. Is it long or short? Thin? Thick? Coarse or fine? Neat or tousled? What color is it? Or colors? Has it always been that color? Has it always been that style?

Or is your character bald? Has your character been bald as long as you have known him or her? If not, when did this character go bald? Is there a particular reason for the baldness? A medical reason, perhaps? Personal choice? Does your character's baldness give you a clearer sense of the shape of her or his head? What is it?

Let's focus on your character's eyes. If you can see their color, what color are they? Even if you can't see it, you may be able to sense it. Are they dark? Light? Are they hooded? Open? What do they reveal? What do they conceal? What do you sense of his or her soul through those eyes?

Now, look around the eyes. Do you see lines of worry? Do you see lines of stress or aging elsewhere on his or her face? Is the face smooth or wrinkled? Tanned and leathery? Or light and porcelain?

If this person wearing makeup? What kind? What does the makeup — the amount, the type, the way it's applied — tell you about her or him?

If this is a teenage or adult male, does he have facial hair? What kind? Is it trimmed or unkempt? Has it changed since the last time you saw him? How?

I asked earlier that you let your shoulders drop. Does your character? Does he seem to carry the weight of the world on his shoulders? Or is she relaxed?

Now look at this person's hands. You can tell a lot about someone from her hands, from his fingernails, from what she is holding in her hands and how she is holding it, from what he is refusing to touch.

Many of the things you are remembering, learning and/or discovering through this experience may never end up in your final draft — or even in your first draft. Regardless, they can offer memory triggers that will help you go deeper in your journey of remembering and re-telling.

Now, this individual begins to walk, if he or she can. Be aware of the individual's gait. Is it strong and confident? Loping? Limping? Hesitant? Long strides? Tiny steps? Is she pigeon-toed? Is he bowlegged? Does she walk with ease? Is he using a cane or crutches? Is she barefoot or wearing shoes? What kind of shoes? Socks? If this individual can't walk, is he in a wheelchair? Bedridden? Where?

Now it's time to engage with this individual. Insert yourself into the scene now playing out in your mind's eye. Go for a walk with your character. Sit down over a cup of coffee or a pot of tea. Join her in one of her favorite activities. Let him take you to one of his favorite places. Let him take you to a secret place. Let her take you to a sacred place.

This encounter can play out in one of several ways. It can be an actual experience you two once shared. Or it can be a something that never happened but that reveals to you something significant about this person and your relationship with her or him. As well, you can engage with this individual as who you are today. Or you can engage as who you were at a time in your past.

Take a few moments for this encounter to play out, however it plays out. As it does, feel free to ask questions and be open to whatever answers you hear or sense. Pause the recording now; restart it when you are ready to continue.

Before you and your character say goodbye, ask one final question: something you didn't think of before or something you were afraid to ask. Be prepared to be surprised by the answer.

Now, thank this person in whatever way feels appropriate to the situation and to your relationship. And as you prepare to part, take one last look at her or him and notice something you missed earlier. However subtle or obvious, this "something" is significant and reveals a quality, characteristic or piece of information that you didn't previously know, realize or remember.

Take your leave from this individual and become aware once more of your physical breath and your physical body. Be aware of your hands. Be aware of your feet. Move your head. Yawn, stretching your mouth as wide as you can.

When you feel ready, open your eyes, be fully present with all you saw, felt, sensed and experienced, and write whatever in this moment calls to you to be written.

Painting the Places of Your Past

Recall as much as possible about the places of your past. Revisit the ones you can. Even places that are now markedly different than they were years ago can evoke a flavor of their past. Regardless, use personal or family photos to trigger your memory of how they were, or look online or in your public library for images that will kindle your powers of recall. Use all your senses to reacquaint yourself with their sounds, smells and textures. With their essence and spirit. With their character. Then use those same Impressionist word paintings we have talked about previously to give your readers just enough detail to feel as though they were present there with you.

As with your description of people, your description of place can be as central to a particular story as is its chain of events. Nor must your descriptions of people and places be segregated from each other. Here's an example from *Acts of Surrender* where they come together as an integrated whole.

> It was a fall afternoon in 1980. Mount Royal's oaks and maples had already burst into fiery display and a chill had begun to cut into Montreal's balmy Indian summer. Gripping his ever-present cup of coffee, David motioned me to follow him into his office. Bishop Court had already begun to empty out.
>
> "Close the door," he said furtively.
>
> David's windowless burrow crackled with electricity, as though its heavy wooden beams anticipated the great revelation that was about to unfold. David didn't smile as he sat me down and settled in behind his desk. But his eyes were bright with excitement.

Physical description is important, but so is emotional memory. Remember how places felt and how you felt about them.

Take yourself back in time to not only see what was obvious but what was subtle, to sense what, perhaps, was invisible.

Here are four techniques to help you go deeper with your descriptions.

1. VISUALIZATION

Close your eyes, get into a meditative space and see yourself walking or driving through a setting from your past. Now see yourself floating above it. Now see yourself looking up from beneath it. How else can you view it? Note the differences each perspective offers you.

Allow your explorations to reveal the unseen as well as the seen, the less desirable as well as the attractive. Visit immediately before or after the time frame of one of your stories. If a particular setting makes multiple appearances in your memoir, visit it at various times and be aware of any differences.

See it all, employing all your senses, physical as well as spiritual and intuitive.

2. IMAGERY

Use imagery to deepen your sense of place, describing it in ways that employ not only sight, sound, taste, touch and smell but all sensory possibilities, including the numinous and otherworldly.

As you do, give your senses free rein. Don't ask only what a place looks like. Ask what it sounds like, what it smells like. If this place were a taste or a flavor, what would it be? If it were an animal or a bird, which animal or bird would it be? If it were a color or shape, which would it be?

Don't forget to use your intuitive and visionary abilities — we all have them — to tune into the spirit and essence of each place.

3. POINT OF VIEW

Certain settings in our past are as significant as the people who populated them. If one of your locales has character-like significance, explore it in a similar fashion on the Muse Stream. Here are some examples.

"I am the house I grew up in. When no one is home, I..."

"I am the Paris of my honeymoon. I..."

"I am my freshman high school homeroom."

"I am the room (or other place/space) that witnessed my first kiss."

You can also write about a place from someone else's point of view for a fuller sense of its depth and relevance.

4. Lists

Create a checklist of attributes and characteristics, or use "Reawakening Your Memory: The Places," which follows. From a place of openness and surrender, run through each attribute and characteristic and allow your memory of its specifics to emerge...easily. As in all your writing, go with first thoughts and don't second-guess what emerges.

If you start with the list I have created for you, feel free to revise it, eliminating elements that don't matter and adding ones better tailored to your life and story. Experiment by writing on the Muse Stream from any responses you get.

Reawakening Your Memory: The Places

Use this checklist to spark your memory about the places that show up in your life story. Don't try to answer each question for each place. Instead, treat this as an exercise in remembering aspects of certain settings that you might have forgotten and in discerning which descriptions might enhance your story.

Of course, not every item will apply to every place in your story, nor could any list ever be exhaustive. For each locale, use what is relevant at the time(s) it appears in your memoir. Take notes if you choose, or simply let the list reignite your recall and rekindle your senses.

Location

- General (region, city, town, etc.)
- Specific (street, road, etc.)

Pace of Life

- Hurried / Frenzied? Leisurely / Slow?
- Urban? Rural?

Time

- Date (specific or approximate)
- Season
- Time / Time of day

Weather & Climate

- Temperature

- Aridity / Humidity
- Type, quantity, quality of precipitation, wind, cloud, sun, fog

Exteriors — General Topography

- Altitude
- Flat? Rolling? Hilly? Mountainous?
- Rocks, cliffs
- Barren? Lush?
- Bodies of water: Ocean, river, lake, stream, swamp, marsh, puddles
- What is just out of view?
- Relevant sights, colors, sounds, smells, textures

Exteriors — Immediate Natural Environment

- Space where the story takes place
- Neighboring area
- Middle- / Long-distance views
- Trees, flowers, grasses, shrubs, other plants/plantings
- Natural growth? / Planted by humans? When?
- Lushness / Sparseness / Health
- Soil color, type, moisture/dryness
- What is just out of view?
- Relevant sights, colors, sounds, smells, textures

Exteriors — Built Environment

- Age, condition
- Building where the story takes place

- Neighboring/nearby structures
- Relationship between structures
- Roads, sidewalks, pavement
- Street architecture (benches, lampposts, trashcans, bus stops)
- Signs
- Middle- / Long-distance views / What is just out of view?
- Relevant sights, colors, sounds, smells, textures

Exteriors — Vehicles

- Cars, motorcycles, bicycles, scooters (including models)
- Buses, trucks, vans (including models)
- Farm/industrial vehicles (including models)
- Pushcarts, shopping carts, wheelbarrows
- Baby carriages/strollers
- Animal-drawn vehicles
- Other vehicles
- Age, condition
- Visible drivers, passengers
- Relevant sights, colors, sounds, smells, textures

Interiors — Vehicles

- Type
- Age, condition
- Relevant sights, colors, sounds, smells, textures

Interiors — Indoor Environment

- General look, style, state, condition, age

- Furnishings, floor coverings
- Wall hangings, art, photographs
- Knickknacks
- Light (quality, source)
- Windows, window coverings
- Plants, flowers
- Food, drink
- Anything else?
- Relevant sights, colors, sounds, smells, textures

INTERIOR — INDOOR CLIMATE

- Comfortable? Uncomfortable? How?
- Aridity / Humidity
- Temperature
- Relevant sights, colors, sounds, smells

PEOPLE & ANIMALS

See also "Reawakening Your Memory: The People"

- Ages
- Genders
- Types
- Sizes
- Clothing
- Hair
- Facial expressions
- Activities

MISCELLANEOUS

- General atmosphere, ambience
- Normal v. unusual
- Visible v. invisible
- Public v. secret
- Numinous/supernatural/sacred

DOMINANT SENSORY STIMULI

- Sights
- Colors
- Tastes
- Smells
- Sounds
- Textures
- Spirit

SECONDARY & SUBTLE SENSORY STIMULI

- Sights
- Colors
- Tastes
- Smells
- Sounds
- Textures
- Spirit

Stepping into Place
A Guided Meditation

Let this meditation help trigger your recall of specific events as well as your sensory memory of the places involved. Not every question or suggestion will apply universally, nor could an experience like this cover every type of location. As with the list earlier in this chapter, ignore what doesn't apply to your story and fill in whatever is missing.

Allow at least 35 minutes for this meditation and for the writing experience that flows from it.

Close your eyes, take a few deep breaths in, and let them go. Inhale deeply. Breathe it all out. Feel your shoulders drop with your breath. Feel your whole body relax.

Allow your breath to travel through your body, massaging all those areas that feel any stress, any tension, any discomfort, and let your breath ease all the physical knots and smooth out all the jagged edges of your emotions.

Let your breath carry you deeper now, and deeper still. Let it carry you into the heart of your story, whichever one of your stories this is for you right now. Breathe into it and allow yourself to feel it. Allow yourself to sense it. Allow yourself to be carried to a place within it.

If this is your first experience with this meditation, it is best to not choose a specific place but to let a place call you to it. It may or may not be the place and time you would prefer to travel to in this moment. It doesn't matter. What matters is that you open to the experience that presents itself to you and that you trust yourself, your feelings, your sensings and your intuition through that experience. This experience.

So let yourself be dropped into one of the places where your story is set. A place and a time. Breathe into that place and time and take a breath or two to reorient yourself to this new place and time and to engage your senses in whatever now surrounds you.

You could be inside or outside. You could be in the far distant past or more recent past.

It could be day or night; spring, summer, winter or fall. So the first thing to notice is where you are and when you are.

What is this place? Do you remember it? Or is it unfamiliar? We will come back to the specifics of it, but for now simply look around and take in all that you see, hear and smell. An overview. Slowly turn 360 degrees and notice anything that is different from what you first saw.

Where are you? When are you? If you can and it's relevant, note the year, month and day. Note the specific time or general time of day. Note the season.

I can't ask you questions that are too specific because the range of possibilities for where you find yourself is too vast. Infinite, even.

But as I ask what I ask, remember to engage *all* your senses. To note what things look like...what things sound like...what things taste like... what things smell like. To reach out and experience touch and texture.

Be specific, naming types, brands, models, styles, colors...noting shapes and sizes. Be aware of the age and condition of what you see. Note what things remind you of, what memories or associations they trigger. Be aware too of the quality of what you are seeing, sensing and experiencing. The physical quality, of course. But also the nonphysical, sensing quality.

Cross your senses, imagining what something you wouldn't normally taste might taste like if it had a taste...what something that makes no sound might sound like if it could make a sound...what something invisible to the eye might look like if it made itself visible...what something you can't reach might feel like to the touch.

As always, pay attention to your nonphysical senses. Trust your gut, your instinct, your intuition. Trust your emotional response.

Let's begin with the out-of-doors. If you're inside and you can step outside, do it. If you can't step outside but can look out a window, do that. If neither is possible, intuit answers to my questions.

Now that you have stepped outside, what is the first thing you notice? Is it something you see? Smell? Sense? Whatever it is, be with that sensation for a moment and know or intuit what that tells you about this place and time.

Get a sense of your surroundings and of the significance of this particular place in your story. Even if your story takes place entirely indoors, you and the other people involved may be affected by what's outside, so look around take it all in. See what you see. Sense what you sense. Remember what you remember.

The same is true of the weather. It may not be directly related to the events of your story, but it can set a mood or tone that can help to more fully engage your readers. Take note of it.

Is the weather normal for this time? This place? This situation? If not, why not and in what way? Does it support you and the events of your story? Or does it create barriers, delays or challenges? Or opportunities?

What is the weather like? Is it cold? Warm? Dry? Humid? Damp? Sunny? What shade of blue is the sky? What is the sun like? Or the moon and stars if it's nighttime?

Is it overcast? Perhaps it's raining. Or sleeting? Or snowing? Hailing? How heavily? How big are the raindrops, snowflakes or hailstones? What kind of clouds do you see? Is it windy? Stormy? What's the wind like? What kind of storm is it? Is there thunder? Lightning? What does the thunder sound like? Is it near or distant? What about the lightning? What does the air feel like?

What about the light? What is that like? The sun casts a different kind of light at different times of day and in different seasons. The phase of the moon affects the quality and availability of light at night. How does the light feel? What mood or moods does it trigger?

Now turn your attention to your surroundings — both the natural and man-made. Note trees, grass, flowers and bushes, both wild and domestic. Note rocks, boulders, mountains and hills. Note buildings and other structures. Note roads, sidewalks or pathways. Be aware of water — everything from puddles through creeks and streams to rivers, lakes and oceans. And be aware of what is on the water and in the water, and what its shoreline is like.

Note sounds. Note smells. Reach out and touch something. What is its texture?

Is there anything you notice that is particularly emblematic of this place?

Are there animals around? Birds? What do they look like? Sound like? Are they healthy and content? Or sickly? How do they relate to this environment? How do they relate to you?

What about people? Although we're not focusing on people in this experience, I would still like you to notice what you see and sense of any who might be present and to note what their presence reveals about this place and time.

Be aware too of vehicles and other conveyances. Cars, trucks, buses, bicycles, scooters and motorcycles. Strollers, baby carriages, shopping carts, pushcarts and wheelbarrows. Airplanes, helicopters and hot-air balloons. Drones. Farm equipment and construction equipment. And in less modern settings, carts and carriages pulled or pushed by animals or people.

Note a vehicle's speed. Also note its color, model, age, condition and anything unusual about it, as these things can also reveal information about the character of the driver. A 75-year-old grandmother speeding through town in a flashy, fire engine-red Ferrari is markedly different from one who is gratingly grinding gears as she inches down the street in an aging rust bucket.

Similar differentiations can apply to everything you see — the buildings, the natural environment, the pavement. So, again, remember to put *all* your senses to work, including sound and smell, and be open to what those senses reveal to you of what might be going on both directly and beneath the surface of this place.

What are you standing on? Grass? A meadow? Gravel? A bridge? A road or path? If so, what is the road or path made of? What kind of bridge is it? Take a step. What is the sound of your shoe or bare foot on the ground? Every surface will sound different. What does this surface sound like?

Continue to look around and be aware, fully, of all the specifics of color, texture, smell...of things that belong, of things that don't belong. Of things that are natural, of things that are in some way man-made or unnatural. Move around, too, if that will reveal more to you.

Look beyond your immediate surroundings to what you see in the middle distance and out to the horizon.

What are you aware of that is hidden from view? Has it been hidden intentionally?

Now step inside and do with the inner space all that you have done with the outside space. Even if your story takes place out-of-doors, enter into a nearby structure and practice your en-visioning skills on this new environment.

Where are you? What kind of space is this? What kind and type of structure is it? Residential? Commercial? Industrial? Retail? Something else?

Is it new? Old? Well-kept? Shabby? Neat? Dirty? Austere and anti-septic? Richly appointed? Comfortable? Utilitarian?

Is it large, spacious and airy? Cramped and tiny? Claustrophobic? What about the windows? Are there windows? If not, what does that feel like? If there are, are they large with expansive views? Or small and prison-like? Perhaps they are even barred.

Notice colors. Smells. Sounds. Textures. And light. What is the light like? Is it natural, from a window or skylight? Or artificial? What's the color and quality of the light? Is it direct? Diffuse? Bright? Dim? Or is there no light at all?

And furnishings. What kind of furnishings do you see here? Note the style and period. Note age and condition. Are they comfortable? Again, notice colors and textures and what they tell you about this place.

Is anything hanging on the walls? What do they tell you? Are there plants? Knickknacks? Is there anything unusual? Eccentric? Out-of-the-ordinary? Unexpected?

Are there books, magazines or artwork? What sort? Are there CDs or DVDs? LPs? What genre? Photographs? Recent or archival? Color or black-and-white? Sepia?

Look in closets, cabinets and drawers for more clues to this room's story and history and to the stories and histories of its owners, inhabitants and occupants — including the you you were then.

What goes on in this room? And what, in your story, has happened or will happen in this room?

Absorb all that this space has to show you, to share with you, to remind you of. Sights. Sounds. Smells. Tastes. Textures. What do your nonphysical senses tell you of the world of this room?

Now move into adjacent rooms and engage with them in the same way, using both your senses and your sensings to discover and uncover both the obvious and the subtle, the in-view, the partially hidden and the fully concealed.

Of course, it's not possible for me to go into every detail of every possibility. So take a few moments to be aware of things that I haven't mentioned specifically, things that are unique to this place and time, things that are especially relevant to your story.

Once again, moving beyond your physical senses, what does this place feel like? What does your gut tell you about it? What does your instinct tell you? Your intuition? What do your emotions tell you about this place? What do you remember about it now that you had forgotten?

If this place were a person or an animal, what kind of personal or animal would it be? Don't think about it. Whatever first leaps to mind is its perfect representation for this exercise.

If this place could speak, what would it say to you right now? If it makes sounds other than words, what would those sounds be?

Before we bring this experience to a close, walk through this place one final time. Step outside again if that feels appropriate. Take a final look around. Notice anything you might have missed previously.

Know that you can return at any time to this place and pick out other things that you missed...pick out new feelings that you aren't now aware of. You can come back at a different of time of day, a different season, a different year, a different point in your story. For no place remains the same through time. The same is true of seasons.

You can also come back to this place as an invisible observer — of a younger you, of other people involved in your story or of both, to see how they interact with each other here and to see what this place is to them, means to them, how it treats them, how they treat it. Their relationship with it.

One final experience before you leave: I would like you to conjure up in some way the essence of this place. I would like you to listen to its wisdom about itself. Let it speak to you, either in words or in the feelings you get from it. Let this place, from its innermost soul, reveal something of itself to you. And as you might do with a person, ask it what it's biggest secret is. Allow yourself to be surprised by the answer.

Now, knowing you can return whenever you choose, bid this place and time a grateful goodbye and allow yourself to begin to feel yourself leaving that place and returning to this one, knowing that all you experienced, whether recorded on paper or not, remains within you, ready to be used in your memoir when the time is right.

Once more, be aware of your breath and feel your body in this time, in this place. Move your fingers. Move your toes. Move your head. And when you're ready, open your eyes, be present and write about your experiences.

6. Envisioning Your Memoir

Vision is the art of seeing things invisible.

Part of the process of writing is not so much
to explain your vision but to discover it.

What's Your Vision?

DO YOU HAVE A VISION for your memoir? What purpose do you hope it will serve in your life and in the lives of others? Perhaps you already know. Perhaps you don't. In either case, a vision statement can help.

If you don't yet have a vision, crafting a vision statement will bring your memoir's aim and intention into clearer focus. If you do, reading your vision statement before you sit down to work with your memoir will keep you aligned with its energy, theme and focus through the entire process of conception, creation, revision and release.

The vision statements I have created for my books have often served as part of my gear-change from the outer to the inner, from mind-focus to Muse-focus, and have ensured that all I wrote hewed as closely as possible to the book's true essence.

A vision statement is not something you think about or plot out. It's something you feel. It can be as brief as a sentence or as long as a page. It can speak in broad terms about your role as writer or memoirist or in more specific terms about your memoir's purpose — in your life, in the lives of your readers, or both.

Nor are vision statements fixed in stone. As your memoir progresses and you mature through the writing of it, you may feel called to refine your vision statement to match new insights and awareness.

On the next pages you will find the vision statement I wrote for *Acts of Surrender*, as well as "Vision Quest," a two-part guided meditation to help you connect with your vision for your memoir and to guide you into creating your own vision statement.

My Vision Statement for *Acts of Surrender*

Acts of Surrender is an exploration for me and an inspiration for its readers.

It is designed to open readers to the possibilities of freedom in their own lives and to the gifts of surrender.

It's about a life not lived without fear but in spite of fear, a life lived in surrender to a higher imperative, a life lived as the Fool in the tarot lives: in faith, and trusting (not always with evidence) that all is good, all is safe and all is provided for.

As I write, I let my stories reveal their innate teachings through the telling of them.

My job is to keep interpretation to a minimum.

My job is to recount and relate, to reveal and recapitulate, to walk the earth naked once more, clothed only in the truths that have revealed themselves to me through the living of them.

I open my heart to this story, my story, more baldly and boldly told than through any parable, as powerful as such telling can be and is.

I open my heart and reveal my vulnerabilities and fears (and, yes, revel in them) so that others may feel free to reveal, revel in and move through theirs.

Acts of Surrender is about the consciousness of freedom through surrender, awakening and revealing itself in the hearts of all those it touches.

Vision Quest
A Guided Meditation

Allow at least 45 minutes to complete both parts of this meditation and for the writing exercise that follows each part.

A professionally recorded version of this two-part meditation is available for streaming or download as part of The Voice of the Muse Companion: Guided Meditations for Writers. *It is nearly identical to what follows. See "How to Use This Book" in Section 1 for details on how to access the recording, as well as for tips on how best to use this book's meditations.*

I. Imaging Your Work

Relax. Close your eyes. Let your hands fall to your lap if you're sitting, to your abdomen if you're lying down. Breathe...deeply...in and out...in and out...in and out.

If you are setting off on this journey any later than first thing in the morning, run back over your day on fast-forward, and every time you get to something that was harsh or jarring, be it a thought, word or action — yours or someone else's — breathe in deeply and blow it out. As fully and noisily as you dare. As many times as you need to.

Just blow it out.

And any moment that was particularly wonderful, breathe it in deeply and reconnect with the energy of that.

Continue to breathe, deeply, and focus on your eyes. If you wear glasses or contacts, imagine, for a moment, perfect vision without them. Imagine unassisted clarity without correction. Breathe into that.

See white light around your eyes and your third eye, that chakra or energy center that lies between your eyebrows and above the bridge of your nose. See that white light cleaning, clearing and cleansing any blurriness, fuzziness, distortion. Feel all veils being pulled away, one by one by one by one. As each veil dissolves, your vision becomes clearer and clearer and clearer.

Now, without removing all your attention from your eyes, move some of your focus to your heart. Be aware of the veils that surround your heart, whatever form they take. Simply be aware of them. Don't judge them.

Now, taking a deep breath, let the outermost veil fall away. Feel it fall away and dissolve. And when you breathe in again, notice that your heart feels lighter and freer and clearer.

As you breathe in again, another veil falls away. And another. And another. Feel how much lighter your heart feels, how much freer your heart feels.

It's okay if it feels a bit scary. Just feel what you feel. Know that you are safe.

Keep breathing and feel yourself grow lighter and freer, lighter and freer, as you move closer to the heart of the matter and closer to who you are as the writer you are, as the memoirist you are.

And what a wondrous place that is.

Once more, breathe in, and if there is another veil there, breathe it away. And the next. And the next. And the next, until all that remains is a brilliant light no longer veiled and dimmed in your heart. Breathe into that and feel it.

Now, let the light from your eyes and the light from your heart connect in a ring of light that circulates energy from eyes to heart and around again. Either clockwise or counterclockwise. It doesn't matter. Whichever way it happens is perfect for you. However the light moves for you, allow yourself to sense it, to feel it. Your vision and your heart as one.

Now, see a second ring of light, moving in the opposite direction from the first, this time connecting your heart to the hands resting on your lap or abdomen. Again, be aware of the circular motion of this circulating energy. Around and around. A constant and consistent river of radiance.

Connect the two rings and you now have a figure eight or infinity symbol within you, as this inner light arcs from eyes to heart...heart to hands...hands to heart...heart back to eyes. And again. And again. And again, creating an infinite, luminous flow with your heart as its center.

As the energy circulates through that figure eight, be aware of the light pulsing in the topmost tips of your fingers, the hands with which you create, the hands that form part of the channel that brings your worlds into reality...that carries your past into the present...that transforms your memories into memoir.

Perhaps you feel the pulsing. Perhaps you don't. Whatever you feel physically, know that the energy is there, the light is there. The creative power is there — in your fingers, in your hands, in your eyes and in your heart, as the flow continues.

Sit with that flow for a few moments, feeling yourself immersed in its river of light and in the creative power that is moving through you.

Now move your focus away from the infinity symbol and back to your eyes, your heart and your hands. Let a beam of light radiate out from your eyes, another beam of light from your heart and a third beam of light from your hands — all meeting at a point in front of you, in front of your heart.

That point in front of you, connected to you by all that light, is your work as a writer, as a memoirist.

If you have written before or plan to continue writing after you have finished this memoir, then perhaps it's your entire body of work. Or it could just be the memoir. Or a single aspect of the memoir. It doesn't matter. Whatever feels right in this moment, let that be whatever it is in this moment.

So your work stands separate from you but connected to you, in that space where all the beams of light meet immediately in front of you, in front of your heart. There is your writing. There is your memoir.

I'm going to ask you some questions about your writing. Your answers might apply to all your writing or only to your memoir. It's not up to you to consciously choose which. When it comes to your individual answers, I want you to allow the first thought that comes to mind to be the answer. As well, I want you to know that you will remember your answers long enough to get them on paper, if that's where they need to go.

So, focusing the beams of light that travel from your heart, eyes and hands and onto that writing space in front of you...

If your writing were a color, what color would it be? Just let the color come. Note it. Don't judge or analyze it. Be with it. Know that in this moment, that color represents your writing. Be with that color for a few breaths.

Now your writing is a space, shape or image. What is that space, shape or image? Again, don't judge or analyze. Let it be what it is. See it if you can. Note it. Know that this too you will remember long enough to write down or draw, if appropriate.

Now your writing is a sound. Music, perhaps. What kind of sound, what kind of music is it, for you, in this moment? Breathe into that sound. Be part of it and one with it. Let it surround you and enfold you, filling you with its melodies and harmonies, with its simplicity or complexity. That sound, however it is, whatever it is, is part of you. You will remember that too, when and if it comes time to put it to paper...or sing it, if that is how you choose to express it.

Now, use your sense of smell. What does that tell you about your writing, about who you are as a writer? Is it a sweet smell? A smell that reminds you of something? Again, just be aware of it, and let it be.

One final sense: What would your writing taste like if you could taste it? Perhaps there's a particular food or type of food. Maybe it's a chocolate sundae, rich and creamy. Maybe it's comfort food — mashed potatoes and gravy. Maybe it's fresh, baked bread. Maybe it's a juicy pineapple. Maybe it's sweet and flowing like honey. Maybe it's spicy... tangy...tart. Let it be what it is. Acknowledge it. Be with it.

Now go deeper still and let one word emerge that captures the spirit and essence of your work. Let it be the first word that comes, whatever it is. Don't judge it, don't analyze it. Don't second-guess.

If it makes no sense to your conscious mind, perhaps that's just as well. Let it be.

Now, staying in this meditative space that you're in, pause the recording and jot down some notes about what you have experienced — the color, the smell, the taste, the shape, the word...particularly the word.

Or take the word that just came to you and write on the Muse Stream from the phrase, "My writing [or 'my memoir' or use its title if you know it] is [insert your word]..."

When you're done, put your pen down and, without reading what you have written, restart the recording, close your eyes and continue.

2. Your Vision

Reconnect with that energy, that space. With that triangle, that pyramid of light. Again, begin to feel the light connecting your eyes and heart and hands with your work, your work as the writer you are...as the memoirist you are.

Now that you have experienced your writing from each of your senses, move your directed focus away from those specific senses.

Stand above them. Get an overview of all that you experienced, all the different connections you felt with your writing through sensing your writing.

From that vantage point, look down at that space in front of you where you and your writing come together, and breathe into that space for a few breaths.

Feel the fullness of it and the vastness of it. The specifics of it too. Feel all of it. Be all of it. Know all of it for the first time, again.

Feel, too, your connection with that part of you that is the writer and the writing and the work. Feel it and breathe into it. Breathe deeply into it.

Now, answer these questions...

- What is it that, deep inside of you, you want to convey through your work? First answer. No thinking about it. Let the answer come freely.

- What is it you want people to experience through your work? Again, go with whatever comes up first. Don't censor. Don't judge

- What do you want people to experience of you through your work?

- What do you want people to experience of themselves through your work?

- Open your eyes, again pause the recording and jot down your answers to some of those questions, to whichever questions were answered.

Remember not to judge or analyze. Simply record your experiences, the answers you have received.

Stay in a meditative space and when you're done, restart the recording. Turn to a fresh sheet of paper or to a clean screen on the writing application on your computer or mobile device. At the top of the page, write: "I, [your name], am a writer. Through my writing [or 'my memoir' or your memoir's title], I..."

From that opening, write on the Muse Stream, letting what follows be as long or as short as it needs to be.

When you are finished, sit quietly in the energy of what you have written before reading it. If possible, read it aloud.

As you continue working on your memoir, revisit and revise your vision statement to keep it current.

7. Editing Your Memoir

Only amateurs think their writing is perfect.
Erica Jong

When you write a book, you spend day after day scanning and identifying the trees. When you're done, you have to step back and look at the forest.
Stephen King

Why Edit?

NO MATTER HOW GOOD the first draft of your memoir is, chances are it is not ready to be sent out into the world. It probably isn't ready for a spouse, partner, curious family member, sympathetic friend or beta reader either.

Thing is, first drafts are messy. First drafts are muddled. First drafts are jumbled. Whether or not you have written on the Muse Stream, your memoir's first draft is certain to be littered with the frenzied chaos that Margaret Atwood describes in "Your Story Knows Best," in Section 2.

Every first draft needs editing. For that matter, every second and third draft also needs editing. Fourth drafts too.

Why?

As you rewrite, edit and revise, you

- Fix typos, correct spelling and tidy up grammar and punctuation

- Eliminate redundancy and ensure consistency

- Rectify factual errors

- Discern what works and what doesn't in each chapter and in the manuscript as a whole

- Minimize your memoir's weaknesses and maximize its strengths

- Make sure your memoir aligns with your vision statement

In short, each draft of your memoir further refines the raw clay of your manuscript into the masterful work it deserves to be and readies it either for self-publication or to be submitted to agents or publishers.

How many drafts do you need? As many as it takes to get your manuscript as good as you can make it. It could take five drafts or fifty. Each manuscript is unique and each comes with its own set of challenges, regardless of your experience and skill level. The original edition of *Acts of Surrender*, for example, took at least six drafts. *Dialogues with the Divine* and *The MoonQuest* each took more than a dozen. Yet *The Way of the Fool* took only three — a feat I am unlikely ever to be able to repeat!

Here's the good news: Your memoir doesn't have to be perfect. In fact, it can't be perfect. Perfection doesn't exist. "Have no fear of perfection," artist Salvador Dali[1] is believed to have said, "you'll never reach it."

If perfection is elusive, excellence is not. However, it takes meticulous, painstaking and committed editing to get there — whether you're J.K. Rowling, Danielle Steel, Stephen King or Jane or John Doe. If you want readers to keep turning the pages of your memoir, if you want your memoir to have its best shot at success, you must edit it through multiple drafts and revisions. As many it takes.

Just so you know, should you go the agent-publisher route instead of self-publishing, your revisions are unlikely to end with your "final" draft. Your agent may ask for more revisions before agreeing to submit your manuscript to publishers and a publisher may insist on yet more before agreeing to take it on.

So don't release your memoir into the world yet. Read on, and let this section guide you through a singular revision process that is certain to make your book more publishable and more readable!

---

[1] The quote has also been attributed to scientist Marie Curie.

Finding the Vision in Revision

When we think about editing, we generally view it as a left-brain undertaking, a mental activity that is largely about precision and fine detail. We also tend to describe it with harsh, aggressive language that's almost abusive.

The author, in this conventional view of the process, must always be in charge...must never relinquish control. For example, we talk about *forcing* the work to our will, about *hacking away* at our writing or about *hammering* our manuscript into shape. If we're editing a novel or short story, we argue that we must *rein in* our characters or, worse still, *gag* or *restrain* them. Such language disrespects not only our manuscript but ourselves as its creator.

I prefer to take a whole-brain approach to editing, one that marries left-brain detail with right-brain intuition and discernment. It's a radical paradigm that views the editing process as one of "re-Vision," of revisiting your original vision for your memoir and putting all your heart, art, craft and skill into aligning what's on paper with that vision.

As you edit, revise and rewrite your memoir, see yourself as a jeweler, delicately etching your rough stone into the jewel that reflects the vision your heart has conceived and received, then lovingly polishing it until you achieve the look and texture you desire.

Your vision is the light force of your memoir, the life force of your memoir. It is the spirit that is its essence, the breath that keeps it alive. Your vision is your dream for your memoir, the expression of your intention. It is what guides it, drives it and propels it — from conception to completion and beyond.

The more deeply you stay connected to that vision, however broadly or specifically you have drawn it, the more completely your finished work will remain true to that life force, that dream, that intention. And the truer you will be to the memoir that has called upon you to commit it to paper and breathe life into it.

TRY THIS

As I pointed out in "Envisioning Your Memoir," working with a vision statement is a powerful way to stay aligned with your memoir — all the way through your revisions to your final draft. If you haven't yet created a vision statement, now would be a good time to do so.

Your vision statement can be as simple as getting into a meditative space and writing on the Muse Stream from the phrase, "My vision for my memoir <or *your memoir's title*> is..." or "My memoir's vision for me is..."

Alternatively, allow your work to speak about itself, writing on the Muse Stream from a phrase like, "I am *<your memoir's title>*. I am about..." Or use the "Vision Quest" meditations in the previous section to guide you.

Whatever your choice, allow to come whatever comes, whether it speaks in metaphor, in general terms or with the most specific of detail. The length doesn't matter. The form and language don't matter. Your conscious mind's understanding of what you have written doesn't matter.

What matters is that at some level you and your creation sing the same song and that that harmony supports you not only as you write but as you refine and enrich your original draft and all the drafts that follow.

Your First Step

Before you launch into your memoir's first revision and any subsequent draft, revisit your vision statement. Don't merely read it. Feel it. Embody it. Connect with it and, through it, connect with the essence of your work.

If possible, read your vision statement aloud — with heart, power, confidence and intent. Thus empowered, the words of your vision statement will fuel and inspire you as you move through each draft and each revision.

Don't abandon your vision statement after you have released drafts of your memoir (or the final book) out into the world. Hold to this vision when you receive feedback, criticism and reviews — positive or negative. This vision, as embodied in and by your vision statement, will always keep you centered and aligned with the true heart of your work.

Now that you have revisited your vision, it's time to revisit your memoir.

The Art of Heartful Revision

1. Take Your Time

Let your work sit quietly for a time before you launch into revision — especially if you are feeling hypercritical and can't help but judge what you have written. That waiting time could be a day, a week, a month or six months after you complete a draft. And it could be longer or shorter from one draft of your memoir to the next.

Even if a publisher or editor is pressuring you to finish, don't panic and don't rush. Your memoir deserves you at your best, and your readers deserve the best from you. Always give both yourself and your memoir the space and distance necessary for you to approach your work heartfully, objectively, respectfully and discerningly.

2. Use Your Whole Brain

Don't rely solely on the logical, detail-oriented side of your brain when you edit. Using your whole brain and body will allow you to see beyond obvious errors and to correct more than surface issues.

Does a sentence, paragraph or chapter not feel right? Does some elusive something about one of your stories feel "off" in some way that you can't identify? Is there some aspect of your memoir that feels as though it doesn't belong? Do you have a nagging sensation that something is missing from one of your stories? Does something else feel out of whack? Trust those feelings, whether they pop into your head or you feel them somewhere in your body. The more you do, the more those intuitive sensings will alert you to problems in your manuscript and the more clearly they will offer you solutions.

As you become more adept as a writer, more in tune with your memoir and its vision, and more in touch with your Muse, you will gain an easy, innate knowingness of what works in your manuscript and what doesn't, without always being able to articulate why. That sixth sense will also direct you to the appropriate fix or improvement — again, often without explanation. Your intuition will never lead you astray. It is the voice of your vision and the voice of your memoir.

3. TALK TO YOUR MEMOIR

As I wrote in "Your Story Knows Best" in Section 2, your memoir knows itself, its story and its imperative better than you do. Listen for its voice and let it tell you where the problems are in your manuscript. Listen with your heart and trust what you hear — in terms of your book's content, shape, theme, format, language and structure. Your memoir knows best, at every stage of the process. The more you "consult" it, the easier your revision journey will be and the truer to your vision your final book will be.

If you need help connecting with the voice of your memoir, revisit "The Spirit of Your Story, the Essence of Your Book" in Section 2.

4. READ ALOUD

We are always more attuned to the rhythm and flow of our language when we read aloud. We often read more thoroughly when we read aloud. You will want to read your work silently as well, of course. But particularly at the beginning and each time you make major changes, your voice will tell you where you have strayed off course.

5. ACCEPT THAT LANGUAGE IS NOT PERFECT

As you revise, never hesitate to seek out more forceful and evocative ways to translate your vision onto the page. (More about that in the next chapter.) Be aware, though, that translation is an art and that language can rarely more than approximate emotion and experience. Think of the most wondrous visual you hope to include in your memoir and imagine trying to recreate that in words. You can come close. Yet whatever your mastery of the language, you cannot recreate every nuance of your vision, emotion and experience. That's okay. Accept the creative perfection of that innate imperfection and...

6. Do Your Best

Do your best to write the words and paint the images that most accurately reflect your life and its stories. Do your best to commit your vision to paper. Do your best to polish, enhance and enliven your memoir so that it aligns with that vision. Do your best with each draft and when it's time, declare it finished and let it go.

7. Suspend Judgment

Judgment is a blunt instrument. Discernment is a more delicate tool: a marriage of intellect and intuition, heart and mind. Heartful revision is about discernment, not judgment. We all judge ourselves and our work too harshly at times. Notice your judgment, but don't give in to it. And don't let it get in the way of your editing.

Feeling judgmental? The guided meditation at the end of this section ("The Spirit of Heartful Revision") will help you edit with more clarity and less judgment.

8. Respect All Your Drafts

Revision is not about taking a machete to your manuscript. It's about treating each draft as a necessary stage in its growth toward maturity. Just as you gently, sometimes firmly, guide your children toward the fulfillment of their unique destinies, guide your memoir with that same spirit of respect — for yourself as its creator as well as for your creation, which has its own vision and imperative.

No word you write is ever wasted. Each word is an essential part of the journey toward a completed draft, and each draft is an essential part of the journey toward a completed memoir. Respect your initial draft. Respect all your drafts. Don't be a slave to them. Allow your work to grow, change and mature, and...

9. Be The Writer You Are

Each draft of your memoir will teach you, and from each draft you will mature in your art and your craft. Strive for excellence, which is achievable, not for perfection, which is not. Be the writer you are.

10. Don't Obsess

Through every stage of your experience with your memoir, there will be infinite opportunities for you to obsess about one aspect or another of the process. Don't do it.

11. Be True To Your Vision

Hold your vision in your heart and mind as you revise, and do your best to align all your edits and rewrites with that vision.

22½ "Rules" for Revision

1. THERE ARE NO RULES

In revision as in writing, there is no single right way to edit your book that is guaranteed to work every time. There is only the way that works for you *today*.

I emphasize "today" because what works for you in revising one project or draft may not always work on the next. So be open, be flexible and remember to use your whole brain.

2. BE SPECIFIC...BUT NOT TOO SPECIFIC

There's a reason why Rule #2 for Revision is nearly identical to Rule #6 for Memoir-Writing: Now is the time to look for those descriptions that still aren't specific enough.

What make and color is the car? What does it smell like? What kind of flowers are in the bouquet? What shapes are the clouds? What is the texture of your grandmother's skin?

This is also the time to dilute or delete any unnecessary detail. Give your readers the specifics that will bring your story alive, but don't overwhelm them with superfluities.

3. SHOW, DON'T TELL

Use detail and description to spark your reader's imagination. Don't tell me that Aunt Mary was a fussbudget. Show her *being* a fussbudget. Don't tell me that the boss at your first job was an ungrateful bastard. Describe him in a way that communicates those characteristics.

4. USE IMAGERY...BUT DON'T OVERDO IT

As you reread and revise your manuscript, look for opportunities to increase or fine-tune your use of imagery. What do things smell and taste like? What do they sound like? What is their texture? Cross senses for more powerful imagery. Ask what the wind tastes like, what the earth sounds like...what someone's face feels like, what an emotion smells like, what your heartbeat looks like.

Connect your readers with the sensory power of your stories, but don't overstimulate them. Imagery used wisely will always enhance your memoir. Imagery used gratuitously will only disrupt your flow and bore your readers.

5. PAINT WORD PICTURES THAT DRAW ON RELATED IMAGES

For the title of Rule #5, I chose words like "paint," "pictures," "draw" and "images" to create and reinforce a particular idea. Would it have been as strong had I written, "Use word pictures that tap into related ideas"? You multiply the power of your imagery when you build on related images to describe something. When one image in the series breaks from the theme, you weaken your overall picture. As with any other tool, be careful not to use it to excess.

6. ADOPT THE RHYTHM METHOD

The rhythm and music of your language show up not only in your choice of words and use of imagery but in how you structure your sentences. A series of short, simple sentences, for example, can build suspense. Longer sentences slow the reader down to a more leisurely pace. Does the type and length of your sentences support the scene you have written and the mood you wish to convey?

Know the effect you want and use the rhythm of your language to achieve it. Reading aloud, as I noted in "The Art of Heartful Revision," can help you hear what is and isn't working.

7. GET ACTIVE (UNLESS YOU NEED TO BE PASSIVE)

When you write with the active voice, the subject of your sentence performs the action: "The dog [the subject] bit Tommy." The active voice is simpler and easier to read than the passive voice; it's also more direct, impactful and, according to studies, more memorable.

With the passive voice, the subject *receives* the action: "Tommy was bitten by the dog." The passive tends to be vague, awkward, stilted and wordy. It also obscures responsibility for the action by removing its source: "Mistakes were made." Unless you are seeking to create an aura of mystery and wish to focus on the unknown ("the jewels were stolen"), get active!

8. Employ Forceful Nouns And Verbs

Adjectives and adverbs can be crutches that hold up sickly nouns and verbs. Find evocative verbs and nouns that stand on their own power and kick away those crutches. Even when adverbs and adjectives help you paint a more expressive picture, seek out forceful nouns and verbs to accompany them for more potent and descriptive writing.

To help you find the nouns and verbs (and adjectives and adverbs) that will enrich your narrative...

9. Make Friends With A Thesaurus

Use a thesaurus (in revision, *not* in writing) to replace adjectives with robust nouns and adverbs with dynamic verbs. Use it, too, to find adverbs and adjectives that more eloquently and effectively reflect your intent. As with any friendship, don't abuse your relationship with your thesaurus. Use it as a tool, not as a crutch.

10. Keep It Simple

Be simple. Be direct. Avoid four- or five-syllable words when words of one or two syllables work as well. In simplicity lies power. Don't drown your reader in flowery excess. Don't show off. Remember Rule #8. If you need help keeping it simple, remember Rule #9.

11. Cut The Fat

Are there words, phrases, sentences or scenes that detract from the essence of your memoir, that weaken your theme, that fail to illuminate your vision? Either delete them or rework them to strengthen your vision.

Have you unintentionally repeated scenes or stories? Have you accidentally described the same person or place multiple times? Eliminate redundancy.

Have you used two or three words — or sentences or paragraphs — where one would do? Seek out ways to say more with less. Remember Rule #10.

Look for words like "very," "actually," "really" and "quite." More often than not, actually, they are really quite unnecessary.

12. FILL IN THE GAPS

You have written, "It was a beautiful day." What was beautiful about it? How did it make you feel? What did it smell like? What did it sound like? Describe it. Add flesh to your skeletons. Illuminate your scenes with detail and emotion.

13. BEWARE UNINTENDED MEANINGS

Could your sentence be read two different ways with two different meanings? For example: "My boss spoke about sex with Frank." Rewrite it so that we know whether your boss was talking to someone else and the topic was sex with Frank or whether the boss was talking to Frank and the topic was sex. (Both Frank and your boss will appreciate it!)

14. CLEAN UP INCONSISTENCIES

Have you placed a single-location story in Burbank on one page but in Los Angeles five pages later? Did your Grade 3 teacher start out as Miss Moss in one chapter, only to become Mrs. Moss in the next? Inconsistencies like these can easily creep into your memoir, especially when you are relying on memory and writing rapidly on the Muse Stream. They can also be easy to miss, especially after multiple drafts and read-throughs. Clean 'em up!

15. Convert Your Clichés

Clichéd writing is lazy writing. Clichéd writing is impotent writing. Clichéd writing is dull. Replace platitudes, hackneyed phrases and overused metaphors with original writing that provokes, astounds and astonishes. If you need help, revisit Rule #8.

16. Seduce Your Readers And Leave Them Wanting More

The first and final sentences are the two most important sentences in any book, including your memoir. A compelling opening sentence grabs your readers (including prospective agents or publishers) and doesn't let them go. And your book's closing sentence, like the final note in a symphony, cannot fall flat or it risks leaving readers feeling cheated and unsatisfied. Make *all* your sentences count, of course, but pay special attention to your opening and closing as you revise and finalize your manuscript.

17. Listen to Your Dialogue

As I mentioned earlier, it's okay to manufacture dialogue, as long as you remain true to the spirit and intent of the speaker and of the situation. After all, no one's memory can perfectly reproduce a conversation from decades past. The key is to write dialogue that sounds life*like* not *true*-life. That's because actual speech is nearly always fragmented and rambling. (Record and transcribe any unscripted conversation if you don't believe me.) Still, it's a good idea to pay attention to real people speaking, not to duplicate the content but to get a sense of the rhythm, music and spirit of their language. And always read your dialogue aloud. It will help ensure that what you have written sounds natural and coherent, not wooden or disjointed.

18. File Away Your Favorites

The sentence you love most, the description you consider unparalleled, the story you cannot bear to cut: These are your favorites, and you may have an unhealthy attachment to them. View them objectively, from a place of loving detachment. Look at them in light of your vision. Ask your memoir if they belong in the book. If they don't, file them away for later use — in a future memoir or fictionalized in a short story, novel, screenplay or stage play. And should you find no future home for them, don't despair. As I noted in "The Art of Heartful Revision," no word you write is ever wasted. Each word, whether it travels the full journey to publication or is left by the side of the road, is integral to the journey.

19. Step Into Your Readers' Shoes

What have you not explained to your reader? Are there holes in your narrative that ought to be filled? Are you making assumptions based on your intimate knowledge of the story, its settings or its players? Unless you are writing to a very specific audience, your readers may need more description, explanation and/or clarification than you have provided. Ask yourself the questions your readers will — and answer them.

20. Allow Your Readers Their Own Experience

What have you over-explained? Are you telling readers too much? Are you going into unnecessary detail? Your readers are smarter, more knowledgeable and more imaginative than you think. You don't need to spell out every moment in your day. You don't need to itemize every one of your experiences. You don't need to describe in detail something that is common knowledge. Give your readers some space.

21. You Will Make Changes That You Will Regret: Get Over It

It's easy, during revision, to make changes in one draft that you regret in the next. To avoid losing your pre-corrected text, create a new document and printout for each draft. If you must make changes within a particular draft, keep the original text visible by enclosing your change in square brackets or by displaying it in a different font or color. If your writing application allows you to revert to a previous draft, enable that feature. And if you have access to a backup system or service that saves multiple versions of a document, like Apple's Time Machine, use it to retain access to those earlier drafts.

22. YOU WILL REGRET MISSING MISTAKES YOU COULD HAVE CORRECTED: GET OVER IT

There will be errors you will miss. There will be errors that editors and proofreaders will miss. Regardless of the number of times you read your manuscript and have it read by others, including by professionals, typographical errors, factual faux pas and other mistakes will slip through.

When you discover them after publication, make note of them so that you can correct future editions. Then let them go.

22½. THERE ARE NO RULES

Every stage of your memoir-writing experience is creative, and every creative act is about innovation, free-thinking, breaking new ground and breaking old rules. Find your own way...in your first draft and in all your drafts.

The Spirit of Heartful Revision
A Guided Meditation

Use this meditation before you sit down to edit. It will help get you out of self-judgment and into the spirit of heartful revision. Have your manuscript handy so that you can go directly from the meditation into editing.

Allow 5-10 minutes for the experience.

A professionally recorded meditation similar to this one is available for download or streaming.[2] See "How to Use This Book" for details on how to access the recording, as well as for tips on how best to use this book's meditations. Note that the recorded version is longer than this one and focuses more on avoiding judgment as you write than as you edit.

Breathe. Breathe in the quiet, white light of your creative essence, your divine essence, your Muse. Breathe in your fire, your flame, your being-ness, your God-self. Breathe in the light of who you are, the truth of who you are, the love of who you are. Breathe in all the light and aloha you are.

Aloha is not merely a word that conjures up the gentle swaying of palm trees and hula dancers. Aloha is a consciousness, a state of being, a state of openheartedness, a state of love in its truest, fullest sense.

Breathe into that openness within you. That love within you. Breathe it in fully, deeply, completely.

Breathe out any doubts, any fears that you're not good enough, that someone else or anyone else is a more accomplished author or creator or has lived a life more worthy of chronicling. Breathe that out, for it is not relevant. Comparisons are never relevant.

---

[2] Search the relevant site/store for "Mark David Gerson judgment"

So let go all feelings that you're not good enough. You are.

Release all feelings that others are better than you are. They are not.

Put aside all feelings that others have lived more memoir-worthy lives than you have. They have not.

You are equal to all and equal to the joyful task at hand, which is about taking the words and passions of your heart that exist in written form as your memoir and sculpting them into finished form.

Not from a place of judgment. Not from a place of "less than." Not from a place of "not good enough."

From a place of humility and self-empowerment. From a place of self-worth. From a place of celebration.

So as you prepare to read what you have written, as you ready yourself to move into and through a new draft of your memoir, breathe out judgment and breathe in discernment.

Breathe out blind criticism and breathe in perceptiveness.

Breathe out harsh self-talk and breathe in compassion.

Breathe out insecurity and negativity and breathe in optimism, hope and heartfulness.

Breathe out comparisons with other writers and with other books, and breathe in the light and essence of your vision.

Breathe out censorship and second-guessing and breathe in the unique expression of your unique life.

Breathe out your mind's perceived need to control and breathe in mindful surrender to the essence of your memoir, to the higher wisdom of your memoir.

Repeat aloud after me:

I <your name> surrender to my highest vision for my memoir, to its highest vision for itself and to its highest vision for me.

As I read, reread, edit, rewrite and revise my memoir <or title of your memoir>, I do so with without fear and without judgment, making only those changes that will enhance the story and stories I am telling.

I now stand ready to shape my memoir into the masterpiece of a gem it deserves to be and that I deserve it to be.

And so it is.

Take another deep breath in as you anchor within you the statement you have just affirmed. Breathe into your commitment. Breathe into your heart. Breathe into your memoir. Take another deep breath, in and out, and now another.

And when you feel ready to approach your manuscript with an open mind, generous heart and discerning eye, open your eyes and reach for it to begin a new round of revisions.

As you do, let a keen eye and an open heart guide you, and let the deepest, innermost knowingness of your intuition pilot you through not only this draft but every draft...all the way through to the moment when you hold your memoir in its final, published form in your hands.

8. Freeing Your Memoir into the World

You just have to say, "To hell with you, I ain't scared of you."
Otherwise they've won.

Salman Rushdie

I don't try to guess what a million people will like.
It's hard enough to know what I like.

John Huston

"What Do You Think of My Memoir?"

AT A CERTAIN POINT on your journey with your memoir, you will want to share all or part of it with a friend, family member or writing colleague. Writing is a solitary pursuit, so it's natural to reach out for feedback and ask, "What do you think of my memoir?" or "Is this how you remember that event?"

Feedback can be either helpful or disruptive. It can either foster your creative process or cripple it. How do you ensure that others' views and comments support your writing project? By always following these Seven Be's of Empowered Feedback when you share your work with *anyone*, including with your life partner, your best friend, family members mentioned in your memoir or members of your writers' group.

The Seven Be's of Empowered Feedback

1. Be Protective

You have no more right to knowingly expose your memoir-in-progress to influences that could harm it or set it back than you do your child. This is especially true if you have felt creatively blocked in the past.

Seek out only those people and situations that will support you and your book. Never assume that those closest to you will be the most supportive. Often, without intending to hurt you, they are the most critical and least helpful.

Always use your discernment and don't be shy about saying no, when appropriate, to someone who asks to read all or part of your memoir. Just because someone shows up on the pages of your memoir doesn't mean that he or she is the best person from whom to seek feedback.

2. Be Open

Your work, like your child, requires fresh air and outside influences. Don't be overprotective and suffocating. Don't let your fear hold you back from sharing your work and vision. Be open to others' perceptions, comments and responses, even as you exercise your discernment in determining which of those perceptions, comments and responses is relevant and appropriate at any particular stage in your creative process.

3. Be Aware

To everything there is a season. During different phases of your journey with your memoir, you will be ready to hear different things. Respect where you are and seek only the type and depth of feedback that you are prepared to receive and integrate. Recognize when you are at your most raw and respect that too. As always, discernment is key.

4. Be Clear

Be clear within yourself about the type of feedback that you require and desire in this moment and on this draft. For example:

Do you want to know which emotions your work evokes? Whether your reader found one of your stories funny? Touching? Compelling?

Do you want to know whether readers found your descriptions, imagery or settings vivid? Original? Credible?

Do you want a friend or family member to compare your version of events with his or hers? Don't forget Empowered Feedback Be #1: Be Protective. Remember too that you are entitled to your version of events.

Do you want detailed line-by-line input? Or do you want only general comments? Or perhaps you seek nothing more than a pat on the back for having completed a first draft, for having told a particularly challenging story...or simply for having written.

It is up to you to determine what will support your creative process at this time with your memoir and what might damage it, so...

5. Be Explicit

Once you have discerned the type and depth of feedback that is appropriate for you and your memoir right now, ask for it — clearly, directly and with neither apology nor equivocation. Your reader cannot know how best to support you unless you make your needs clear. Don't be shy or embarrassed to make those needs known. If you are vague, hesitant or unclear, you open yourself to comments that you may not be ready to hear, comments that could feel hurtful or damaging, even if they are not intended to be so.

6. Be Strong

Know what you want and don't be afraid to speak up — lovingly, compassionately and, again, without apology — when you aren't getting it, or when you are getting something you didn't ask for. This is your memoir and your creative process. You have every right to seek out what will help and support you as you bring your book to completion. In this, you are not only training yourself to determine what will assist you, you are training your friends, family and fellow writers to provide feedback in supportive ways and to seek it for themselves in empowered ways.

7. Be Discerning

The words on your page are an expression of you but they are not you, even as they chronicle aspects of your life. Negative comments, whether intentionally cruel or not, have no power to harm or stifle you unless you allow yourself to be hurt or blocked.

In fact, take neither praise nor criticism too seriously. Deep inside, you know your memoir's strengths and weaknesses. Tap into that intuitive knowingness and rely on it to discern which comments it is wisest to ignore and which support you and serve your memoir at this stage in its development and yours.

ASK YOURSELF THESE QUESTIONS

- How can I be clearer within myself about the feedback I require right now and with others about the feedback I am seeking?

- How can I be more discerning about where and to whom I turn for feedback?

- How can I be more respectful of my work's needs and my own when seeking feedback?

- How can I be more discriminating in determining which feedback to take to heart and which to dismiss?

"Read This Before You Read My Memoir"

Before you pass your memoir to friends, family members or fellow writers for feedback, ask them to read these Seven Be's of Compassionate Feedback, and satisfy yourself that they are comfortable abiding by them.

The Seven Be's of Compassionate Feedback

1. Be Open-Minded

You don't have to agree with the writer's history, lifestyle or version of events in order to offer constructive feedback. Nor is it your place to comment on them, unless asked. Respect the writer's life, approach and views. If you don't feel that you can, suggest, respectfully, that the writer look elsewhere for feedback.

2. Be Constructive

The only reason to offer feedback is to support the writer and his or her work. This is not a test of your ability to pick out errors or flaws in the memoir, nor is it an opportunity to criticize the writer's life situation and choices. Don't judge. Be open-minded. Don't be smart. Be compassionate. Don't show off. Be constructive.

3. Be Balanced

Always begin with the positive — with what you like about the memoir, with its strengths, with what works for you, with what you admire or respect about the writer's life and story. With that foundation of support, you can then begin to offer constructive comments. Frame whatever you say with respect and compassion, and honor the parameters the writer set out when asking you for feedback.

4. Be Specific

You are at your most helpful when you can offer examples from the text of what works and what doesn't. Be concrete. Be clear. Be fair.

5. Be Respectful

Give only the type and level of feedback the writer has sought. If there are other elements that you would like to comment on, ask permission. Respect the answer you get.

6. Be Nurturing

Sometimes all a writer needs is praise for having written. Avoid the kind of question Nora Barnacle is said to have asked husband and *Ulysses* author, James Joyce: "Why don't you write books people can read?"

7. Be Compassionate

Hew to the Golden Rule of Feedback: "Speak unto others in the manner you would have them speak unto you." Put yourself in the writer's shoes and offer feedback as you would *honestly* prefer to receive it.

Ask Yourself These Questions

- How can I listen more clearly to the nature of the feedback that has been requested of me?
- How can I be clearer and more specific in the feedback I offer?
- How can I be more respectful of the memoir and its author, offering feedback that doesn't show how smart I am but, instead, serves the needs and growth of the writer and his or her work?

From the Annals of the Infamously Rejected

The literary world is littered with later-regretted rejections. My favorite, not because it's the most extreme but because it involves an author whose work and life have profoundly influenced mine, involves Madeleine L'Engle, author of the young adult classic, *A Wrinkle in Time*.

L'Engle received two years' worth of rejections from twenty-six publishers for *A Wrinkle in Time*, which, once it was finally published in 1962, went on to win major awards and be translated into more than a dozen languages. Madeleine L'Engle was hardly unique...

- J.K. Rowling was rejected by a dozen publishers before Bloomsbury accepted the first Harry Potter novel and only, legend has it, because the chairman's eight-year-old daughter insisted.

- Publishing giant Alfred A. Knopf rejected Jack Kerouac's *On the Road*, dismissing it is as a huge, sprawling and inconclusive novel that would attract small sales and garner indignant reviews. Knopf also rejected George Orwell's *Animal Farm* ("it is impossible to sell animal stories in the USA"), as well as Sylvia Plath ("there certainly isn't enough genuine talent for us to take notice"), Anne Frank, Isaac Bashevis Singer ("it's Poland and the rich Jews again") and Vladimir Nabokov.

- Kurt Vonnegut, William Faulkner, Judy Blume, Jorge Luis Borges ("utterly untranslatable"), Norman Mailer ("this will set publishing back twenty-five years"), James Joyce and D.H. Lawrence also received multiple rejections before finally getting a yes.

- Stephen King's *Carrie* was rejected thirty times, leaving the author so discouraged that he gave up on it, tossing the manuscript into the trash. Fortunately, it was rescued by his wife.

- Other literary rebuffs? William Golding's *Lord of the Flies*, Oscar Wilde's *Lady Windemere's Fan*, Joseph Heller's *Catch-22*, Anita Loos's *Gentlemen Prefer Blondes*, John le Carré's *The Spy Who Came in from the Cold* ("you're welcome to le Carré — he hasn't got any future"), Kenneth Grahame's *The Wind in the Willows* ("an irresponsible holiday story"), the original "Tarzan of the Apes" short story by Edgar Rice Burroughs and F. Scott Fitzgerald's *The Great Gatsby* ("you'd have a decent book if you'd get rid of that Gatsby character").

- Publisher Arthur C. Fifield cruelly parodied Gertrude Stein in his 1912 rejection of *The Making of Americans*: "I cannot read your M.S. three or four times. Not even one time. Only one look, only one look is enough. Hardly one copy would sell here. Hardly one. Hardly one."

Toward the end of her demoralizing two-year period of rejections, Madeleine L'Engle covered up her typewriter and decided to give up — not only on *A Wrinkle in Time* but on writing. On her way to the kitchen, she had an epiphany: an idea for a novel about failure. In a flash, L'Engle was back at her typewriter.

"That night," she explained three decades later in a PBS documentary, "I wrote in my journal, 'I'm a writer. That's who I am. That's what I am. That's what I have to do — even if I'm never, ever published again.' And I had to take seriously the fact that I might never, ever be published again. ... It's easy to say I'm a writer now, but I said it when it was hard to say. And I meant it."

ASK YOURSELF THESE QUESTIONS

- Can I refuse to let my fear of rejection prevent me from finishing my memoir?
- Can I refuse to let my fear of success prevent me from finishing my memoir?
- Can I refuse to let criticism, negative feedback or rejection stop

me from moving forward with this memoir or with any other writing project?

- Can I refuse to let pressure from friends or family censor my memoir or stop me from telling my stories the way I know they need to be told?

- If publication eludes me, can I trust that there may be other reasons why I was called to write this memoir? Can I be okay with that?

TRY THIS

In your journal, write on the Muse Stream from each of these phrases, going as deep as you dare to discover the extent and impact of your fears:

- My fear of failure...

- My fear of success...

- My fear of others' reactions...

- I trust my memoir to...

9. ENGAGING IN THE WORDS OF THE WORLD

A book is proof that humans are capable of working magic.
CARL SAGAN

I have always imagined that paradise will be a kind of library.
JORGE LUIS BORGES

Read to Write, Read to Live

WRITING A BOOK IS MOST OFTEN a solitary act, one that can pull us out of the maelstrom of daily living and into a monastic place of creative retreat. When you're in the midst of birthing a memoir — and even when you're not — it's important to be part of the shared world of creation and imagination inhabited by your fellow authors. Take time to read as much good writing as you can, regardless of form, medium or genre. Here's why...

1. Expansion

Reading, along with all the arts, expands us as human beings, as conscious beings and as writers. Whether you spend time reading memoir or another genre, you will deepen your knowledge of the human experience, including your own, and connect with both the heart of creation and the creator of heart and art.

2. Craft

Osmosis is one of the most powerful learning tools available to the human heart and mind. When we read great writing, we absorb the author's craft and technique. We sense at a deep level what works and what doesn't. Without having to know or understand how or why, without needing to analyze or parse, the power of the words we read finds its way into our writing.

You won't be copying. You will be absorbing, filtering and adapting. You will be learning — in the easiest and most fun way imaginable: by doing nothing other than enjoying another's words.

Once again, genre doesn't matter. Topic doesn't matter. What matters is that you read good writing by accomplished authors.

3. Stress-Reduction and Creativity Enhancement

Reading, researchers at Britain's University of Sussex have found, is one of the best ways to relax and lower stress levels — more effective than listening to music, drinking tea or coffee, going for a walk or playing video games.

The university's 2009 study suggests that even six minutes of silent reading can cut your stress by sixty-eight percent, slowing your heart rate and easing heart and muscle tension.

According to cognitive neuropsychologist Dr. David Lewis, who conducted the study, "Losing yourself in a book is the ultimate relaxation." The words on the printed page, he noted, stimulate your creativity and cause you to enter into what is essentially an altered state of consciousness. "This is more than merely a distraction but an active engaging of the imagination."

4. Blatant Self-Interest

Do you want to be read? Do you want your memoir to find an audience? If you as a writer aren't reading, what sort of example are you setting for your potential readers?

The creative/literary community is not a one-way delivery system. It's a bustling marketplace of ideas and concepts where readers not only learn and grow from writers, but where writers learn and grow from readers and from each other. If we write, in part, to be heard, then we must also be prepared to listen.

Again, genre and subject are less important than engagement, then opening a book — any book — and surrendering to the words and imaginings of a fellow artist.

ASK YOURSELF THESE QUESTIONS

• Why is reading important to me?

- What am I reading right now?
- What books have I read this month?
- What books am I looking forward to reading?

If you aren't reading, visit your nearest bookseller or public library, or browse your favorite online bookstore, and discover the words and worlds that are waiting for you on their real or virtual shelves.

Step beyond the walls of your creative enterprise and engage!

10. YOUR MEMOIR, YOUR LIFE

Remember that writing is translation,
and the opus to be translated is yourself.
E.B. WHITE

You don't remember what happened.
What you remember becomes what happened.
JOHN GREEN

Your Memoir, Your Life

Writing is alchemy, truly a tool of wizards, witches and sorcerers.
It's the magic wand, the incantation,
the wave of the hand that transforms all.

THE VOICE OF THE MUSE: ANSWERING THE CALL TO WRITE

ALCHEMISTS OF OLD WERE SAID to possess unique wisdom and power: They could turn ordinary metals into gold. As memoirists, we do something similar: We take the leaden moments of our past and restore them to the golden light of consciousness through words on a page. In doing so, we are also alchemically transformed.

Even if you have not yet finished your memoir, even if you are still moving through your earliest drafts, you may already be living the tectonic shifts of inner revolution — outer too, possibly — that are inevitable byproducts of the memoir-writing experience.

- What have you learned about yourself over the weeks, months or years of this odyssey?

- What have you discovered or rediscovered about your life through writing this memoir?

- Who are you now that weren't on the day you began this memoir?

- How has your inner life changed?

- How has your outer life changed?

- How have you changed?

In your journal, note whatever answers to these questions leap easily to mind.

When you're finished, turn to a fresh page and answer them again

— this time by writing on the Muse Stream. Don't stop to think about what to say. Don't stop to judge or censor. Be honest. Be open. Be vulnerable. Hold nothing back. Allow yourself to be astonished.

When you're finished this second part of the exercise, ask yourself whether any of these revelations have a place in your memoir — possibly in an afterword, epilogue or other closing chapter. If you sense that they do, take the raw material from your journal and craft the appropriate chapter, being as forthcoming with your readers as you have been with yourself...as the writer-alchemist you are.

My Memoir, My Life

After I completed the main body of my Acts of Surrender *memoir, I did an exercise similar to the one I describe in "Your Memoir, Your Life." The result would morph into "The Next Surrender," the original edition's concluding piece. Here is an excerpt from that piece.*

"From the moment nearly three years ago when I set down the first words of the first draft, this book has remained one of my most profound, and difficult, acts of surrender. As Toshar does in *The MoonQuest*, I have had to overcome my reluctance to write my story or risk a form of stasis. As Q'nta does in *The StarQuest*, I have had to accept the predominant role that storytelling plays in every aspect of my life or risk living without passion. And like Ben in *The SunQuest*, I have had to not only recount my past but re-experience its emotions with sometimes disturbing fidelity, or risk betraying my human potential.

"If I were to choose an archetype to describe my life's journey, it would be the Fool, a tarot character often pictured stepping off a cliff into the unknown. His may be a leap of faith, but it's never blind faith. For he knows that even as he trades the certainty of solid ground for the mysteries of the void, the infinite wisdom of his infinite mind will guide him forward. This knowingness frees him to surrender again and again. And again. Not without resistance and not without fear, but in the conviction that resistance is futile, fear cannot stop him and meaning is always present, even when it is invisible.

"The tarot Fool may appear to have a choice in his folly: In many decks, one of his feet is still firmly anchored. He could step back. Or could he? In my favorite representation, from *The Osho Zen Tarot*, it's too late: One foot hangs off the edge; the other only barely touches the earth. That's the kind of Fool I am: always in motion, with a momentum that keeps pressing me on to the next act of surrender. Any other choice breaks faith with a choice I made long ago, a choice that banished conventional free will from my life, a choice to live my passion as authentically as humanly possible, whatever the consequences.

"As I observe my fears around this new edition, this new coming out, I realize that if Toshar could not move forward until he had set his story onto parchment for all to read, I cannot move forward either, as the Fool that I am, until I take a further step in making mine public. And so I make the commitment — to this next leap of faith, to this next surrender.

"There will be more acts of surrender after this one. There always are. Each one will push me harder than the last. Each one will nudge me closer to my essential truth. Each one will require a greater leap of faith. And through each, I will continue to trust in the story. Whether it's the story I'm writing or the story I'm living, it always knows best."

Mark David's 12½ "Rules" for Living

As you read through these so-called rules for living, they may sound oddly familiar. That's because you have already read a version of them... in the rules for writing I included earlier in this book.

Why are the two lists so similar? Because I don't believe you can separate your creativity from the rest of your life. After all, isn't life the ultimate creative act? If so, aren't you simply translating one form of creativity (your life) into another (your account of that life) through your memoir?

RULE #1

There are no rules: There is no right way. There is no wrong way. There is only your way...the way that works for you today.

RULE #2

What works for you today may not work tomorrow, so you might as well live in the present moment.

RULE #3

Listen to your heart and trust it; it speaks with the voice of God (or whatever you call that divine intelligence or infinite mind we all carry).

RULE #4

Be vulnerable: Share your pain and your passion. That's what makes you human.

Rule #5

Treat yourself as you would treat your child or best friend: with love, compassion and respect.

Rule #6

Don't live your life according to others' expectations...or according to your own preconceptions. Free yourself to follow the path that is uniquely yours, and surrender to its gifts and surprises.

Rule #7

It's not how often you meditate, it's whether you live your life as a meditation.

Rule #8

Giggle. Smile. Dance. Guffaw. Don't take life too seriously. Just as you don't censor your pain (see Rule #4), don't censor your joy.

Rule #9

It's not how hard you push, it's how fully and unconditionally you surrender.

Rule #10

Find your passion and embrace it. Passionately.

Rule #11

It's not about being perfect, it's about being human.

Rule #12

Empower yourself: This is your life. Don't let anyone else tell you how to live it (or how not to live it).

Rule #12½

There are no rules. None. Never.

Even should you commit to following these "rules," will you ever live them perfectly? I doubt it. I know I don't! (See Rule #11.) I've also written a whole book on the subject: *The Way of the Imperfect Fool*!

But to the best of my imperfect ability in each moment, I live as authentically as I can, surrendering as unconditionally as I am able to the truest path I can envision, honoring my passion with each choice and focusing on what I have, not on what I lack.

I write the same way.

11. THE WRITER YOU ARE

*We tend to forget that our real gift is not so much
what we can do, but who we are.*

HENRI NOUWEN

You don't put your life into your books. You find it there.

ALAN BENNETT

You Are a Writer
A Guided Meditation

I INCLUDE THIS MEDITATION *in all my books for writers because it's too easy, as creative artists working largely in isolation, to diminish both ourselves and our output and to forget that we are powerful and empowered creators.*

Listen to this meditation when you feel doubt...when you feel less-than... when you don't believe that you will ever be able to complete your book... when you question whether you are even a writer.

In those moments, let the words and spirit of what follows remind you that you are a writer of power, passion, strength and courage. For writing a memoir is an act of courage...of immeasurable courage. And you are doing it!

Allow 5 minutes for this meditative experience.

A professionally recorded meditation similar to this one is available for download or streaming.[1] See "How to Use This Book" for details on how to access the recording, as well as for tips on how best to use this book's meditations.

Close your eyes and take a few deep breaths as you relax and listen...
You are a writer.
You are a writer of power, passion, strength and, yes, courage. For writing is an act of courage. Acknowledge that courage, the courage that got you to this point...having written. Having written today, if you have. Having written just now, if you have.
You are a writer.

---

[1] Search the relevant site/store for "Mark David Gerson you are a writer"

Breathe into that. Breathe into the release you felt as the pen flowed across the page, as letters formed into words, words stretched into sentences and sentences began to fill your pages.

Breathe into the freedom, the vibrancy, the love. Breathe into the knowledge and knowingness that you can do it again. And again. And again. And again.

You are a writer.

What you write is powerful. What you write is vibrant. What you write, whatever you believe in this moment, is luminous.

Trust that to the best of your ability, in this moment. Acknowledge the writer you are, in this moment. Breathe into that.

Breathe out judgment. Breathe out fear. Breathe out not-good-enoughs. Breathe out comparisons. What others have written does not matter. What you have written is all that matters now, in this moment. It is perfect...in this moment. Know that. Trust that. Breathe into that.

If you don't feel ready to read what you have written from that place of trust, discernment and compassion, set it aside. Set it aside for a time — until you arrive at a place of more clarity, more objectivity, more self-love.

Don't avoid reading it, but nor do you need to rush into it. Either way, for now know that you are a writer. A writer writes. That's what you have done. You have written.

You are a *writer.*

You *are* a writer.

You are a writer.

You've heard the words. Now speak them with me...

I am a *writer.*

I *am* a writer.

I am a writer.

Speak them again and again and again, knowing them to be true.
Speak them again, feeling the truth in them.
Speak them again, for they are true.

Appreciation

My first thanks must go to author Joseph Allen Farris, who, I'm certain, will be surprised to find himself mentioned here. As Joseph was sharing with me the compelling story of how he came to be a writer a while back, I interrupted him and exclaimed, "You have to write your memoir!" In that same moment, my Muse offered me a whispered injunction of its own: "Your next book will be about memoir-writing." And here we are!

Going farther back, to 2000, there would likely not be a *From Memory to Memoir* had Aalia Golden, then my wife, not urged me to surrender to my passion and teach writing again after a too-long absence. One of the workshops I developed at the time — both to rescue me from a job I hated and to jumpstart a stalled writing project — was called *From Memory to Memoir: Writing the Stories of Your Life*, a title I liked so much that I used it for all my subsequent memoir-writing workshops and have now appropriated for this book.

Going farther back still, no book of mine would be complete without an expression of gratitude to my mother, who taught me to love the written word, and to Carole H. Leckner, who, as my first mentor, showed me not only that I could be creative but that it was safe for me to be creative.

Thanks, too, must go to the participants of all my memoir-writing workshops over the years. That you responded so powerfully to my offerings encouraged me to surrender to the voice of my Muse and write this book.

Special thanks to Kevin Truong for the author photo, which was shot as part of his brilliant "Gay Men Project." View the rest of Kevin's pics from that session at www.thegaymenproject.com/2018/11/02/mark-david-writer-portland-oregon, and be sure to check out the other featured subjects while you're there.

I would be remiss if I did not also thank Kathleen Messmer, not only for *From Memory to Memoir*'s evocative cover image but for her unceasing encouragement, support and generosity of spirit.

My gratitude goes out as well to my many online friends and followers: Thank you for cheering me on, on this project as on many others.

Finally, to my Muse: Thank you for fueling my work, my passion and my life...and for continuing to remind me through each of my writing projects that you're smarter than I am!

More Writing Inspiration!

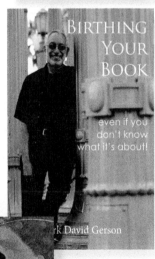

Mark David Gerson's Memoirs

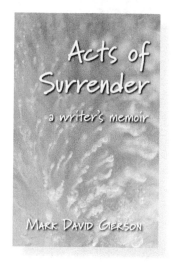

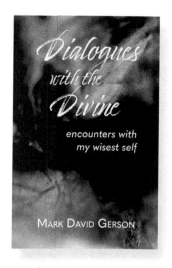

"Positive Inspiration at Its Best!"

Printed in Great Britain
by Amazon

24373861R00118